Boyson on Education

Also by Sir Rhodes Boyson

Speaking My Mind: Autobiography (Peter Owen, 1995)
Centre Forward: A Radical Conservative Programme
(Temple Smith, 1978)
Crisis in Education (Woburn Press, 1975)
Oversubscribed: The Story of Highbury Grove
(Ward Lock Educational, 1974)
The Ashworth Cotton Enterprise (Clarendon, 1970)

Boyson
on
Education

Sir Rhodes Boyson

PETER OWEN

London & Chester Springs

PETER OWEN PUBLISHERS
73 Kenway Road London SW5 0RE
Peter Owen books are distributed in the USA by
Dufour Editions Inc. Chester Springs PA 19425–0007

First published in Great Britain 1996
© Sir Rhodes Boyson 1996

ISBN 0–7206–1019–2

A catalogue record for this book is available from
the British Library

Printed and made in Great Britain
by Biddles of Guildford and King's Lynn

Contents

Foreword

Why is it that after twenty-one years of Conservative Government in the last twenty-six years British education is so far behind the standards of schools in Europe and the Far East?

In the 1930s and the early post-World War II years our education standards equalled those of our competitors, but we fell behind from the 1960s. It seemed that two curses fell on our schools. The first curse was the growth of an egalitarian philosophy which considered that all children, whatever their other differences, had the same intellect and should be taught the same curriculum in the same schools.

The second curse was imported from the USA and threatened the status of the teacher as a teacher. This philosophy considered that it was better to find out rather than be taught, however slow the process. It was in a way the myth of the 'noble savage', that if children were left alone they would cherish learning, decency and all the virtues. The status of the teacher as a teacher was undermined. Thus we had both an egalitarian philosophy and a retreat from structured learning where each teacher and class and even pupil did their own thing. The non-graduate teachers also saw a social and professional advantage to themselves in the comprehensive school and marched behind its banner.

The Labour Party in the early 1960s was looking for a social programme after its economic reforms, and it alighted on the comprehensive school which matched its then egalitarianism. The Conservative Party, feeling strangely guilty because so many of its leaders

7

and Members of Parliament were educated in the private sector, found it difficult to fight for the bright working-class boy who suffered most from the new Labour comprehensive doctrine. Indeed, at the behest of Mrs Thatcher I tried to convince Conservative Harrow to save its excellent grammar schools, including Harrow County School, which was then sending more pupils to Oxbridge than Harrow School, but alas the Conservative councillors there were impervious to reason and were swept along by the comprehensive tide.

I was in a strange position, being the Head of a very successful comprehensive school where we had setting and streaming and academic successes. However, there was no way I could tolerate the new Labour thinking which damaged the bright, working-class boy in the downtown areas, and I moved to the Conservative Party on educational as well as economic grounds.

The comprehensive schools in the up-market areas are basically grammar schools with a slower secondary-modern-school stream, while the comprehensive schools in the inner cities are basically poor secondary modern schools where the bright, working-class child has probably less academic chances than a village boy in the Middle Ages.

When the Conservatives won the 1970 election Mrs Thatcher became the Secretary of State for Education and Science. However, she had no remit from Mr Heath to reverse the egalitarian tide. She saved many grammar schools but the comprehensive tide poured on, often with Conservative local authority support, and in areas like Inner London standards of education practically collapsed. The university Departments of Education and the Colleges of Education became even more left-wing and it is no wonder that we lost the next general election.

When we came back into office in 1979 I was, against my wishes, put in charge of higher education and not schools. We still had no alternative philosophy to the comprehensive tide and the Education Department itself, along with most Directors of Education, fully supported a total comprehensive school policy. As a Junior Minister in charge of higher education I had no direct *locus standi* on secondary education.

Foreword

Against radical left-wing policies the Conservative Party often acts, as Professor Hayek of *The Road to Serfdom* held, as a brakeman and not an alternative driver. When I took control of schools for two years I saved many grammar schools, but the egalitarian tide flowed on, now with a move to one examination at the age of sixteen – again another egalitarian triumph. The Conservative Party, as against Conservative voters, had no will for an alternative policy.

Kenneth Baker, as Minister of Education, bravely tried to turn the tide in 1988. Alas he was, dare I say it, even too radical and the pressure on the schools was too great. But the tide began to change and there was a slow return to standards of excellence, even in many comprehensive schools. At last the left was being challenged on its own grounds.

Mr Major is concerned with content and not structure and he is radical in his view of schools. The idea of doubling the assisted places scheme and the extension of the excellent grant-maintained schools gives those in education confidence for the future. In the grant-maintained schools Mr Major has put parents and teachers in charge, not left-wing administrators. The nursery voucher could also be extended to primary and secondary schools. It is a popular counter-revolution. At last we have a chance to get education right in Britain. This is why I have written this book now. We must control the educational tide; the right has in the grant-maintained schools and the introduction of the educational voucher a perfect combination for freedom and excellence which could transform the education of our country.

What Are Schools For?

Schools have a number of special purposes, which can be summarized as the provision for all children of the opportunities for a purposeful and happy life. For such a life children must be literate and numerate so that they can take a full part in society, both in work and in play. To be illiterate and/or innumerate means that they will be cut off from the means of obtaining information which could be of continuing use to them.

It was alleged that compulsory education was introduced into Britain so that Parliament could educate its masters as the franchise was extended. Employers presumably also wanted more literate and numerate employees if they were to compete successfully in a world economy. Unskilled jobs are now rapidly disappearing and the information technology revolution has already put at risk what were once secure white-collar jobs.

Schools, however, must do more than satisfy employers and politicians. Literacy and numeracy in themselves are avenues to a wider world than the industrial horizon. There must be the teaching of history so that people will grow up knowing who they are, of geography so that they know that there is a great world here and abroad, and of science which has helped to make us master of our environment. Schools must also give children a taste of high culture in literature, art, drama, religion and music which can broaden and uplift the lives of young people.

Schools must also help the home to develop self-control in the growing child and the ability to make friends, to discuss objectively and have a sense of fair play. Schools must also teach good habits of work so that pupils will be able to hold down jobs and support their families and take pride in their achievements. Children must also be encouraged to be aware of their place in the universe and what thinkers and prophets have taught. Man is not an island to him or herself.

Education in the beginning is largely concerned with the development of skills and the absorption of facts and both are exciting ventures for the young. My experience is that children and young people will grow up to challenge orthodoxies, but they must first learn what these orthodoxies are. That is also what schools are for.

Will schools continue into the next century or will the information technology revolution make them obsolete and will parents have to play a greater part in their children's education? I doubt that this will be the case, because teaching is a skilled occupation and children are social creatures who like school and, amazingly, even like examinations.

There will always be the odd parent who educates his son or daughter at home and I would defend his right to do so, provided the youngster sits and passes the national tests for his age group. A good parent teaching his child is much better than the child attending a bad school. It is also the level of attainment and maturity that matters, not the years of automatic attendance.

I spent nearly twenty-four years as a teacher, nineteen of them as a head of three secondary schools. I have sat on education committees and spent four years as an education minister. I wrote for three of the famous, or infamous, Black Papers and co-edited two of them.

I pen this book for my friends – the men and women in the street – who are concerned for the education of their children and grandchildren and the future of our country in an ever more competitive world. They want to know what they can do to help their children.

I also pen it for the tens of thousands of classroom teachers who have to take the heat and burden of the day week in and week out, passing on to their classes the skills and values they will need in adult life. These Mr, Mrs and Miss Chips are the backbone of our educational system and it certainly was not such people who damaged British education.

I thirdly pen the book for the new breed of governors who are giving up their time to run our schools. Between 1979 and 1983, in the Commons Committees and in the House, I advocated that the powers of school governors, rather than those of local education authorities, should be increased. The tens of thousands of such governors can help to rescue British education because they still have innate common sense.

1

Pre-school Education

Britain became the first Industrial Society because we had the coal, the iron, the water, the communications, a partially-trained populace, a seafaring trading tradition and a free market economy. Schools were then opened to provide a higher standard of literacy and numeracy and mechanical knowledge.

Education, however, is the first essential for the new communications age. We need a well-trained flexible labour force working within a free market economy. Education probably starts from the moment of conception when the fertilized egg absorbs from its mother messages and approaches, but I leave that to other more knowledgeable medical pens.

The new-born child soon sees, hears and absorbs much from his environment and the adult world. I believe that when the birth is registered the parents should be given a pack of material as to how they can help their child in the pre-school age and what standard he or she should have reached by the age of five. Parents must be bluntly told what is expected from them.

Parents should be encouraged to talk to their child from the time of birth and should soon start to tell the growing child simple stories. Before very long the child will understand one or two of these stories, which will become his or her favourites to be repeated almost nightly, first by the parents and afterwards by the child. The time will come when the child will want to see the story book and will want to learn the written story so that he can read it for himself. The use of a tape machine at such a stage would be helpful, where little stories can be read and heard and language can be developed. If the child joins a school playgroup there will be further opportunity both for the growth of literacy and speech and also for the exciting world of numbers.

By the age of five the child should be able to dress himself, put on clothes in the right order, go to the toilet and clean himself up. He or she should also know how to use a spoon and a knife and fork. Nose-blowing and washing and drying oneself should also be second nature by the age of five.

The youngster should also know the meaning of the words 'please' and 'thank you'; he should know his name, his address, his date of birth and the location of where he lives. He should know the days of the week, the months of the year and the primary colours, which he should be able to name. He should also be able to count and understand numbers up to ten and be familiar with words like 'lunchtime', 'morning', 'afternoon' and 'yesterday'. Other words like 'tomorrow' and 'first' and 'last' should be mastered. The youngster should also be able to complete a twelve-piece big jigsaw, know how to hold a book, put objects in size order and follow a sequence of pictures in a book. He should also be able to recite at least three nursery rhymes.

Infant school is not play school. It is for teaching English and arithmetic and basic general knowledge, and a pupil who comes into the infant school unprepared for schooling could be handicapped for life. It is up to parents as to how the child attains the necessary knowledge, habits and disciplines to be ready for school study, but acquired they must be.

The early years are the foundation years and without foundations no proper edifice can be built. The curiosity of the young child must be encouraged and trained. Some years ago two scientists in the University of Pittsburgh School of Medicine experimented with cutting off the whiskers of young rats. They found that if the rats' whiskers were trimmed every day part of their brain did not develop properly. The rats needed the experience of touch before the brain could develop and the same happens with young children, who learn by playing with objects. Eyes even only develop from early practice. It is in the early years when proportionally the child makes most progress both physically and intellectually and also learns a code of behaviour.

In 1988 a team from London University led by Professor Barbara Tizard found that children who knew their letters before they were five had a head start over their classmates which still showed at the age of eight and a half. This was true whether they were working class or middle class, black or white.

Pre-school education has only really taken off in this country in recent years. The Cross Commission on Elementary Education in 1888 recognized the need for it and by 1908 half the local education authorities provided some provision for three- to five-year-olds. The Hadow Committee of 1935 called for nursery schools for children from 'unsuitable environments'. In 1995 some 10 per cent of three-year-olds and 45 per cent of four-year-olds were in pre-school nursery places.

Just before the House of Commons recessed in July 1995 Mrs Gillian Shephard, the Education and Employment Secretary, in probably her first initiative in the combined Departments, announced plans for a £1,100 voucher to be given to parents of all four-year-old children with which they will be able to buy a place – probably half time – in a nursery or playgroup with a distinct educational influence. The 20,000 playgroups must be offered the full voucher. The scheme was to go on trial in February 1996 in a number of areas and be fully operable by April 1997, probably the date of the general election, at a net increase in expenditure of £185 million a year. The voucher will be given for the term after the child is four, one year before compulsory school attendance. Parents will be able to top up the voucher where they prefer. Already over half of the three- and four-year-olds attend nursery and primary schools. Parents will receive reports on their children's progress.

I warmly welcome the entry of the voucher into British education. I have advocated the voucher at different ages of education for over twenty-five years. The voucher puts control of education with the consumer (in this case the parent) and not the producer (in this case the local education authority). I also like the mention of the 'light touch' of any inspection procedures instead of the issue of endless bureaucratic rules.

I am not convinced, however, that all children are ready for full-time education at the age of four or even five years. Our children become full-time at the age of five, as against the age of six throughout most of Europe, seven in most of the USA and even eight in a number of its southern states.

As a member of the awkward squad I also do not see why the £1,100 voucher cannot be given to a mother who stays at home and teaches her own child and spends the money on books and teaching equipment. The more we can put the family back together the better, and if a mother can show she is actually teaching her child literacy and numeracy she should be given the full voucher.

Children watching television is no substitute for them talking with their family. Such children can parrot television jingles without understanding them at all. Pre-school television addicts whose parents rarely play with them miss out on word games and the conversation which helps to reinforce understanding. Such children will lack social skills and can become withdrawn video game or computer addicts isolated from social contacts. Children need the traditional games which develop verbal skills and imagination as well as play with model railway engines, dolls and all kinds of appliances. Beware the wealth of technology which can impoverish childhood and hold back the real skills needed for adult life.

The Government's voucher scheme has now been given more substance. It is expected that the children will move towards literacy and numeracy with increased fluency of language and the use of numbers up to ten. Their creativity should be encouraged, their talk improved and the knowledge of the local environment increased. Mention is also made of 'a developing sense of right and wrong'. For this to be effective there will be the need for rewards and punishments. If children are allowed to misbehave in their voucher year and achieve little, then the voucher will be a disadvantage and not an advantage to them and to society. School should be fun but it must be disciplined fun.

Concerned parents who have 'worked' with their children since birth must assess the advantages and disadvantages of the pre-school voucher year, visit different nurseries and playgroups and then decide whether the voucher is for them and, if so, which pre-school arrangement is the one for their child. At its best a year of half-day attendance could be the most advantageous.

In the private sector children are now 'interviewed' as early as the age of three for joining nursery units attached to prestigious schools. The 'right to childhood' seems very tenuous, but small children apparently delight in 'growing up' more quickly.

Primary school governors will be aware that a successful and popular nursery school attached to their infant school will enhance the reputation of their school and act as a recruiting agent throughout its catchment area.

2

The Infant School

The infant school is for teaching English and arithmetic and socializing children in small and larger groups. Infant school teachers are not child-minders, which would be a waste of their training and talents. Children also want to learn and to become grown up, and grown-ups read and write and number. If a child has not begun to read, write and number by the age of seven he or she could easily become a lesson-resister reacting against the teachers and becoming bloody-minded at the approach of adolescence.

"I must confess that I found the national curriculum Key Stage 1 – that is from five to seven years – astonishing. Its pages had almost every truism (apart from 'God is Love') known to bureaucratic men and women. It did have a section, thank goodness, on phonic knowledge but it was too discursive and we had the ritual bowing to Information Technology which is useless without basic literacy and numeracy.

Phonics is a code and a systematic way of teaching reading based on the alphabet and forty letter groups. The alternative methods are 'look and say' where the picture of every individual word has to be learned by heart, and 'real books' where the pupil by luck or osmosis suddenly finds that he can read! Children *may* learn to read accurately by the latter two methods, but for class instruction in schools one needs a system which works for the vast majority of children."

It was the ancient Egyptians who long ago discovered letters which make up words as against the ideogram – the separate picture for

20

each word. The 'look and say' method of teaching reading would take us back to the ideogram! The teaching of reading by means of the child having to memorize the pattern of every word is the equivalent of handloom weaving as against modern automatic looms.

Nearly fifty years ago I trained for teaching at Manchester University, where I chose the course for infant and junior teachers, and I have been interested in the teaching of reading ever since. In 1950, however, when I received my teaching certificate, there was a surplus of junior teachers in Lancashire and I had instead to take a head of English post in Ramsbottom Secondary Modern School in East Lancashire, near my home town. I have always called myself since a 'junior school drop-out'!

This school in its fourth year had a large number of illiterate and semi-illiterate boys who totally fitted the category of lesson-resisters and I had a great struggle to teach a number of them to read. When I first met them they pretended they could read but were bloody-minded, but they knew really that they could not read and I had to win their confidence over a number of weeks before we could actually move to phonic instruction at their age of fifteen. All but one or two could read fairly fluently by the end of the year and their behaviour was transformed.

The decline in reading standards in our country is certainly not the fault of the classroom teacher nor the parents of the children. The fault clearly lies at the door of the so-called progressive educational establishment of inspectors, advisers and departmental officials who for thirty years up to 1979 totally dominated educational philosophy and appointments with their open-plan schools, discovery methods and free discipline.

Teaching children to read is time-consuming and difficult with a new class every year. I have always suspected that so-called modern discovery methods were brought in by inadequate teachers who were also bored by phonic teaching, which is a discipline in itself. Most so-called modern methods were brought in for bored teachers and not bored pupils! To each child starting to learn to read, reading is an exciting process and each advance brings a great deal of satisfaction and sense of achievement.

21

I was taken to the small local Church of England village school at the age of five at the beginning of the school year. The teacher asked who could read. I could read and for the morning I was a hero, at least as far as I was concerned. In the afternoon, however, the teacher tested us in sums and I could not number. The teacher was so cross she knocked me around the room and I cried piteously. That evening and most of the night my mother and father did arithmetic with me and by morning I could number. I have never forgotten that lesson: I feared the teacher's wrath and a repeat of the slapping I received from her the previous day. Corporal punishment may be unpleasant but in school it generally worked.

I firmly believe that all children without brain damage should be able to read and number by the age of seven. As part of the national curriculum I would have a simple written examination in reading, writing and arithmetic which was externally set and marked all over the country, and where the expectation was that all children without brain damage could pass.

The first such test should be given at Easter in the second infant school year. Those who passed would be on the immediate roll of honour to move from the infant school to the junior school that September. The rest of the class would sit again a week before the summer holidays after further tuition by their teachers, and those who still did not pass would have to attend school throughout the summer holidays to be examined again at their end. I would be inclined to bring back for the summer holiday tuition the teachers whose pupils did not pass. I am sure they would pass the following year! It is essential that all pupils without some form of brain defect should have started to read, write and number thoroughly in the infant school.

However, the evidence is that there are now many pupils without brain defects who are leaving the infant school totally unable to read, write and number. This must be the most widespread 'child abuse' in Britain. There is just no point in moving such a pupil to a more difficult class in the junior school when he or she has not mastered the beginnings of the basic subjects. Such pupils will certainly not flower in the junior school.

Overall it appears that standards in the basic subjects have changed little over the last fifty years, apart from a fall in the standards of achievement in English and arithmetic in the 1970s. Dr Joyce Morris, in her 1953 study in Kent, while declaring that standards there were above average for the country, considered that 19 per cent of the children that she surveyed had not made a start in reading at the age of seven. A 1961 survey concluded that 25 per cent of pupils in the infant school at the age of seven had not started to read. John Patten, when he was the Secretary of State for Education and Science in 1992, concluded that one in four children could not read by themselves at the age of seven and one in three could not do calculations as simple as $9 - 6$ and $6 + 2$.

The 7-plus test which I suggest could be more simple than the Government's Standard Assessment Test. They should be simple pencil and paper tests like the Suffolk Reading Scheme or the MacMillan Group Tests and save the time of the class. They should be externally set and marked.

What we need is all pupils in normal schools progressing roughly together and being taught together. The more class teaching there is the better since individual tuition, although occasionally essential, can be a great waster of the time of the teacher.

In 1990 Martin Turner, an educational psychologist, with other psychologists published data covering the 450,000 seven-year-olds which indicated that in the previous five years the number of children with serious reading difficulties had doubled. In January 1995 a report by the Office for Standards in Education (OFSTED) stated that a quarter of seven-year-olds were not being taught the three Rs properly.

A report by the National Foundation for Educational Research has also indicated that on average some forty-seven hours only of a four-year teacher training course is given over to the teaching of reading and that some colleges give fewer than sixteen hours of such tuition. There were also cases where no lecturers on the teacher training course were qualified to teach reading techniques.

I have purposely stressed the difficulties in teaching the three Rs, particularly reading, because these are the very foundations of education and if they are not properly dealt with then the pupil could be handicapped for life. Beyond such teaching, or even in it, the good teacher can make almost anything exciting while the poor teacher can make everything boring.

For interest I have compared the primary education curriculum of 1959, named *Primary Education*, with the new national curriculum. A book could be written on their differences. I find *Primary Education* very down-to-earth and realistic, while the national curriculum is hopelessly vague if earnest. The new national curriculum mentioned Information Technology but did not have an index, which was present in *Primary Education*.

Parents and governors must ensure that their children are being given a full infant school education and that the three Rs are mastered, preferably by the age of seven. Nothing can compensate for the lack of the three Rs, and particularly reading. Similarly the governors should make sure that in their schools priority is given to the mastery of the three Rs. Like a building the foundations are necessary before any ornamental superstructure can be erected.

One last point for parents. I am now informed that one in five children have a television set in their bedroom. My father would not allow a radio in our house until I left to join the Royal Navy and I would not allow a television set until my children were fluent readers. Television, particularly following the decline in standards of programmes over recent years, is basically entertainment and a spatter of unconnected pieces of information. I trust all parents ensure that the purchase of encyclopaedias precedes the bedroom television.

Governors and parents must ensure that the three Rs are taught in the beginning, in the middle and throughout the infant school.

3

The Junior School

I did my two teaching practices in junior schools and apart from sixth-form teaching I consider the most exciting ages to teach are from nine to thirteen years, when the children have settled down in their primary school or lower secondary school, but they still have a sense of awe and excitement in all learning.

In June 1944 the Education Department republished *The Handbook of Suggestions for Teachers*, which was reprinted again in 1957. This handbook was much more specific than the new national curriculum, with many more definite suggestions for teachers according to their age range. It is a pity that these two editions were not reprinted for general distribution; it would have saved a lot of time and money. It was also written in paragraphs with careful headings as against long lists. The paper for the current edition of the national curriculum looks, however, much more expensive!

The main difference between *The Handbook of Suggestions for Teachers* and the 1959 *Primary Education*, as against the current national curriculum, is that the two earlier books, with their clear suggestions, would be of far more use to a new teacher. Perhaps we only needed an updated version of the 1959 primary school book. The difference between the two earlier books and the national curriculum is what is wrong with British education as a whole. This is that present-day suggestions seem often vague and non-specific, while teaching is a specific profession whose primary purpose is the passing on of knowledge. Certainly teaching syllabuses I have seen abroad are much more specific than those now used in our schools. I find time and time again the difference between Britain and the rest of Europe is that the Continent gives specific suggestions whilst the British suggestions are delightfully, or undelightfully, vague. Most countries have agreed syllabuses arising from agreement about the specific aims of education but, alas, in Britain over the last twenty-five years there has not been such a general agreement.

The junior school should extend the skills of reading, writing and arithmetic and give a specific body of knowledge in history, geography, religious education and literature. Sport, art, handicrafts and basic science should also be taught.

A four-year survey of 2,000 children by the Inner London Education Authority in 1986 showed that primary schools where teachers structured their lessons properly, concentrated on the three Rs and awarded stars and certificates for good work had the highest standards. The voluntary-aided church schools, often in the worst buildings, had the best results. Mixed-aged classes had the poorest results. The current Chief Inspector of the Education Department, Chris Woodhead, has stated that a quarter of the lessons in infant schools and 30 per cent of the lessons in junior schools are poor. He added that the teaching of literacy and numeracy, particularly in inner-city schools, must be improved.

The *Sunday Times* in June 1994 reported on the arithmetic skills of young children in 1879 in an elementary school in Harrow. They handled sums like $6,341 + 1,098 + 3,587$ and got the right answers, as against much more simplistic addition at the present time in most junior schools.

A report published in 1995 showed that the worst literacy standards over all age groups were those of recent school-leavers. One in 12 of the 22- to 24-year-olds had low English skills compared with one in 20 of the 32- to 34-year-olds and only one in 33 in the 42- to 44-year-olds. In 1995 the Basic Skills Agency reported that 30 per cent of ten-year-old pupils in junior schools were not able to read properly and that they were likely to remain low achievers for the rest of their lives. Children who have not learnt to read by the age of ten are likely to pretend that they do *not* want to read and, to keep up their self-esteem, they become lesson resisters. Boys in particular from this group can become lesson and school resisters, especially in our inner cities where problems are immense.

Primary school parents must ensure that by home support and close contact with the school their children become both reasonably literate and numerate by the age of seven. Similarly the primary school governors must ensure that the basics – literacy and numeracy – are regularly and competently taught in their schools. Nothing in art, craft or sport can compensate for a lack of confidence in the three Rs and nothing ever will!

The Secondary Heads Association published a report in November 1995 which indicated that the standards of children joining their schools had gone down as compared with the standards of 1991. Part of the blame for this decline was ascribed to the continued changes in the national curriculum over recent years. When 20 per cent of seven-year-olds cannot achieve the expected Level 2 on personal tests for mathematics and reading it is no wonder that there is concern regarding national standards of education.

The first national tests of eleven-year-olds showed that 69 per cent of the 620,000 children sitting the test could not multiply 95 pence by 18 pence without a calculator, and 59 per cent could not work out the cost of seven drinks at 48 pence each and eight drinks at 52 pence each. At the same time I would commend the suggestion of the Chief Inspector of Schools, Chris Woodhead, regarding the advantages of whole class teaching.

I regret that Mrs Gillian Shephard has ruled out the publication of primary school national test results before the next general election. Secondary school improvement has followed the publication of GCSE and 'A' level results of all schools and I suspect that the publication of primary school national test results for each local authority and school would have a similar effect.

I strongly favour the prohibition, or at the least the limitation, of the use of calculators and digital technology in the primary school. The human brain is a muscle and a remarkable calculating machine and as a muscle it must be developed. As in Japan and most European and Asian countries, young children should not be allowed to use calculators. Children must first develop their own number sense through self-calculation or they will never really understand and master arithmetic and mathematics.

Children should be able to 'guesstimate' or they will not be able to know when they have used their calculators wrongly and nonsense answers have been accepted. Children must develop a feel for numbers before they move to mathematical aids. I am glad that it has been agreed that pupils in Key Stage 2 and 3 – that is seven- to nine-year-olds – should have to take a test without the use of calculators to ensure that their basic numeracy is sound.

There has been evidence recently of West Indian families sending their junior school children back to the West Indies because of their disillusionment with British educational standards, particularly in the inner cities. Such parents have to pay the air fares of their children and school fees in the schools in the West Indies, but they are prepared to do so because of poor discipline, modern ineffective teaching methods and possible drug-taking and other criminal activities in inner-city schools.

4

The Secondary School Curriculum

'The greatest part of what is taught in schools and
universities does not seem to be the most proper
preparation for that which is to employ them during the remainder of their days.' ADAM SMITH

I have always been concerned about the curriculum of secondary
schools from the time that I drew up my first syllabus in charge of
English at the Ramsbottom Secondary Modern School in 1950. After
being appointed, the Headmaster suggested I should commence the
following morning and that it would be helpful if we had an English
syllabus. That evening I visited the Headmaster of the Haslingden
Secondary Modern School near where I lived, who was a friend of
my father, and we talked through the English syllabus that he used
and I took it home and typed up an amended syllabus including
lists of books, many of which I had never heard of but with which
over the next five years I would become fully conversant. I arrived
at school the following morning with the syllabus, which took the
Headmaster by surprise, and he decided that he had better keep a
close eye on me. We became good friends, however, but alas I do
not have a copy of that first syllabus that I ever drew up.

The Haslingden Headmaster also recommended to me the *National Handbook of Suggestions for Teachers*. I immediately acquired a copy. This was the 1937 edition, which was reprinted at
the time of the Butler Education Act going through the House of
Commons in 1944. The book ran to 571 pages, covering all subjects,

ages and abilities. It dated back to 1904 and it had amongst its headings: 'Elementary Education is a General Education, Attitudes of Mind are as Important as Mastery of Skills, A Summary of What the School Can Do, The Marks of a Good Education, The Characteristics of a Good School, The Relation between School Life and Home Life, The Maintenance of Discipline, Various Kinds of Grouping in a School, The Function of the Traditional Class, Promotion by Attainment and Promotion by Ability . . .' The handbook then laid down what could be taught in each subject, presuming in the larger schools that the pupils were separated into three streams of ability. I have been very surprised to discover how few current teachers or administrators even knew that this book existed and the amount of sound common sense it contained. As a guide for teachers it was much more definite, down to earth and less verbose than the present national curriculum.

I taught English all the week, apart from one lesson of religious education and some games periods. In 1950 the school-leaving age had been increased to fifteen and this 'reform' was certainly resented by the pupils and staff of the Ramsbottom Secondary Modern School. I had 4C for over six lessons of English and taking charge of this class, particularly as it was taught in an annexe of a delapidated technical school three miles away from the main school, was rather like an initiation in combined operations in the armed forces. My new syllabus certainly did not appeal to them – indeed nothing did – but, as I have already explained, we worked out over the year a *modus vivendi* and parted as friends, and all but two of the boys achieved a reading age of at least twelve before they left in the summer.

From 1950 to 1974, when I left schoolteaching, there were many changes of curriculum. External examinations (which I favoured) and the raising of the school-leaving age (of which I was sceptical) brought changes in the school curriculum. We also had the move to the comprehensive system of secondary schools brought about both for educational and political reasons. There was thus by the 1970s a need to reassess what schools were for and what examinations should be taken. It was just a matter as to which political party took the initiative first. By then I had become fully immersed in the Black Paper movement which wanted a clear purpose in all schools, including comprehensive schools, with the appropriate adjustments of the curriculum and of the power basis in education.

I thought in 1976 that the Labour Party under James Callaghan would take this initiative. He appreciated the validity of many of the views of the Black Paper movement and in his Ruskin College speech of 18 October 1976 he touched a chord recognized by the rest of the country. He said:

It is not my intention to become enmeshed in such problems as to whether there should be a basic curriculum with universal standards – although I am inclined to think that there should be. . . . To the teachers I would say that you must satisfy parents and industry that what you are doing meets their requirements and the needs of their children. There is no virtue in producing socially well-adjusted members of society who are unemployed because they do not have the skills. . . . I do not join those who paint a picture of educational decline because I do not believe it genuinely true, although there are exceptions which give cause for concern.

It did not appear, however, that Shirley Williams, who was then Secretary of State for Education and Science, shared the Prime Minister's down-to-earth views and the Labour Party lost the initiative on educational organization and curriculum which it still has not regained. The 1944 Act was left well behind and it was the incoming Conservative Government of 1979 that began the organizational and curriculum changes which are still with us.

Why did the Labour Party accept what could be called the Americanization of schools to the disadvantage of the working-class children, whom they claimed to represent? I think the partial answer could be the move of the Labour Party at that time towards social democracy as against firm working-class standards. James Callaghan understood this; Shirley Williams did not.

The Conservative Government elected in 1979 began a whole

series of changes in the organization of education and examinations culminating in the 1988 Baker Education Act which laid down a very tight curriculum control on all state schools to an extent never contemplated, never mind enforced, before. However, the full discussion on the curriculum which had been launched in 1976 did not go away. The genie was out of the bottle. The Department of Education and the Inspectorate published a number of discussion and consultation papers on the curriculum from 1977 to 1985. In the latter year Sir Keith Joseph, the Secretary of State for Education, announced that a clearer definition of curricular objectives was required to guide parents, teachers and employers.

Later, in *Better Schools*, we had the ministerial view that 'A more precise definition ... of what pupils of different abilities should understand, know and be able to do, will assist with the formulation of the curricular policies of the Secretaries of State, the LEA and the school; will help all concerned to assess the effectiveness of policies and practice; will encourage teachers to have high expectations of pupils and so help bring about their realisation.' The hand of Keith Joseph can be clearly seen in one other paragraph: 'some awareness of economic matters, notably the operation of market forces, the factors governing the creation of private and public wealth, and taxation, [as] a prerequisite for citizenship and employment'.

Keith Joseph ceased to be Secretary of State for Education in May 1986 and he was replaced by Kenneth Baker. In 1987 we had the *Curriculum 5–16 – A Consultation Document* and the following year the 1988 Education Act was brought in, which I considered then and consider now was over-regulatory in its intentions and in its results. Under this Act there were three core and seven foundation subjects plus religious education. The three core subjects were mathematics, English and science and the foundation subjects were history, geography, technology, music, art, a foreign language and physical education at secondary level. It was intended that the ten subjects should take up 75–85 per cent of available school time. This was cut to 70 per cent of teaching time at the Second Reading of the Bill. I stated then that no national curriculum should take more than 75 per cent of primary school time and no more than 50 per cent of secondary school time. I also stated on the floor of the House of Commons that tests to ensure the national curriculum was followed should be very simple pencil, pen and paper tests to be sat by the children and marked outside the school so that the pressures were not increased on teaching and preparation time.

Alas, warnings were not heeded and complicated and time-absorbing tests intruded on teaching. The curriculum was drawn up by large subject committees chosen by the Secretary of State and assessment took considerable time and was often bogged down in minutiae. Parents and the teacher unions were united in opposing the over-bureaucracy and the time wasting of these tests and in 1993 there was a widespread teacher boycott. John Patten, who was then the Secretary of State for Education, asked Sir Ron Dearing, the Chairman Designate of the new Curriculum Assessment Authority, to review urgently 'the manageability of the curriculum and assessment framework of this year's test . . . particularly taking in the views of serving teachers who have had experience of implementing the national curriculum assessment arrangements'. Sir Ron then sensibly recommended a streamlining of the classroom tests, the scrapping of the seven- and fourteen-year-old league tables, more concentration on the three Rs and the restriction of the test for the eleven-year-olds to English, mathematics and science.

These recommendations were accepted by the Department, including the recommendation that each school should have one day a week – one-fifth of the timetable – entirely under its own control. It was also agreed that there would be no further changes for the next five years. The next year, 1994, showed that a *modus vivendi* had been developed since parents in a Gallup poll indicated that 80 per cent supported the testing of children in mathematics, science and English at eleven and fourteen and 75 per cent agreed that parents should also know the results of all local schools. There is no doubt in my mind that these national tests and the wider parental choice of school could do much to improve British educational standards.

We may now have got the balance right between what is regulated nationally and the freedom of the individual school to develop its own ethos. School governors have now so much more power over their schools and there are tens of thousands more governors. It is essential for them to ensure that the basic curriculum is followed in every school.

It is also the responsibility of both parents and governors to ensure that within the national curriculum there is time and encouragement for individual teachers with special skills to enthuse young people both in and out of lesson time. This balance between freedom and authority is one we all know and its successful achievement makes the reputation of a good school locally, just as its achievement nationally makes a successful nation. Every parent and governor should assist in these aims.

If a school objects to the national curriculum then, with the agreement of the governors, the school can apply to the Education and Employment Department under Section 16 to change to its own curriculum in part or in whole. Grant-maintained schools can apply directly to the Secretary of State. It will be interesting to know the number of schools that do apply.

5

Secondary School Reorganization

From 1950 I was a secondary school teacher. I saw the rise of the comprehensive school movement and its virtual triumph throughout the country. In 1950 there were three types of secondary school: grammar, technical and secondary modern in that order of status. Some 20 per cent of children went to grammar schools, 5 per cent to technical schools and the rest to the secondary moderns.

My first school, Ramsbottom Secondary Modern School, was a typical secondary modern. It was a three-stream old board school, with a central-halled building surrounded by prefabricated huts to allow for the increase in numbers following the raising of the school-leaving age in 1950. No one stayed on beyond the school-leaving age except one boy so that he could play for Lancashire School-boys at soccer. At thirteen there was also the technical school examination for boys only. So boys who sat and failed were twice rejected. The school had a good working-class, small business and shopkeeper intake and I believed that pupils should be allowed to stay on to take external examinations. The Headmaster disagreed so in 1955 I applied for a Headship in the next valley, was appointed and immediately offered extended courses, to the horror of most of the staff and the delight of two or three more understanding teachers who realized that the rigid bipartite or tripartite system was unviable.

I was one of the first headteachers in Lancashire to offer extended courses in secondary modern schools. A Lancashire County official came to see me to deter me from such a course and I then developed a technique which I used on many future occasions.

I listened to the County official and nodded without speaking and as soon as he had left continued with my course of action. The County official thus thought that I had misunderstood him, he returned and we went through the same procedure again, including my ignoring his advice. This time he did not return. Four years later the same County official did return to my school to ask me to lecture to all the Lancashire secondary modern school heads on the advantages of extended courses in secondary modern schools!

In 1959 there was support for the secondary modern school in the Crowther Report, which recommended that abler pupils should also sit School Certificate subjects and that, in conjunction with the raising of the school-leaving age to sixteen, more challenging work should be presented to pupils. Meanwhile, the technical high school had been enthusiastically endorsed by the Norwood Committee, which regarded it as a pathway to university for those with a particular aptitude in mathematics and science. There was not, however, any momentum behind their growth. In 1952 there were only 291 technical schools as against 1,189 grammar schools!

The Labour Party was in the late 1930s vaguely in favour of multilateral schools, but between 1945 and 1951 there was no real challenge to the bipartite or tripartite system. From 1951 to 1964 the Conservative Government limited the growth of comprehensive schools to purpose-built schools, mainly in new housing estates and new towns and the London County Council area. The Conservative Government's White Paper *Secondary Education for All* in 1958 also acknowledged the need for comprehensives in rural areas. By the time Sir Edward Boyle became the Minister for Education in 1962 some 90 of the 163 local education authorities were working on schemes of comprehensive reorganization. The Labour Party came into power in 1964 and issued circular 10/65 in favour of comprehensives and deploring early selection.

I left my Lancashire secondary modern school in 1961 to become Headmaster of the Robert Montefiore School in the East End of London, which was an old central school on which I built a successful sixth form. From there I moved in 1966 to take the Headship of Highbury Grove School, a purpose-built comprehensive absorbing a grammar school, a secondary modern school and a residual school. If I had taken instead of a London school the headship of a rural comprehensive school the likelihood is that I would never have been involved politically in education or in national politics. I arrived at Highbury Grove, however, at a time when education was breaking down totally in the capital, with left-wing cells in many schools determined to destroy not only education but the free society. My move to the right was in response to circumstances.

In 1970 Mr Heath won the General Election and Mrs Margaret Thatcher issued circular 10/70, which basically supported the co-existence of well-established grammar schools with new comprehensive schools throughout the country. Mrs Thatcher did prevent the closure of a number of well-established grammar and secondary modern schools, but by now few local authorities were prepared to defend tripartism and secondary reorganization actually quickened. Attention was now moving to how the comprehensives would be organized. Although this was not obvious to all, by 1970 tripartism and indeed bipartism was dying as far as the country was concerned. Between 1965 and 1970 the number of grammar schools declined from 1,180 to 975 and this decline accelerated between 1970 and 1975 – largely a period of Conservative Government – so that only 547 grammar schools were left by the latter date.

By 1979, when I became an Education Minister, the first Bill we put through Parliament was to restore to local authorities their full right to organize education in their areas according to local wishes, but the bipartite battle was already lost. Between 1981 and 1983, when I was in charge of schools, I saw hundreds of delegations regarding secondary school reorganization and saved a fair number of good secondary modern schools and grammar schools from change, but allowed reorganization where it was obvious that the people in the area wanted it.

One irony is worth mentioning. My father, a Labour Councillor and Alderman for forty years, fought to retain the Bacup and Rawtenstall Grammar School when he was Chairman of the local Divisional Education Executive of the Lancashire County Council. He succeeded! Several years later, when I became an Education

Minister, Lancashire County Council again tried to make this grammar school into a comprehensive and a delegation came to discuss the matter with me. After consideration I turned the application down because of the weight of local opposition to this proposal. I sometimes think that there should be outside this grammar school, which still exists as a grammar school, two statues – a red one for my father and a blue one for me!

The battle regarding the comprehensive school was partially lost by the Conservatives because so many of their rural county leaders had their children in independent schools, about which they felt guilty. Indeed, some were even persuaded that the comprehensive schools were the parallel in the State sector of the independent schools, which would have surprised both sets of headteachers. We have certainly gone a different way to our European partners in secondary school organization, either to their or our disadvantage. So far it clearly seems to our disadvantage, at least educationally.

For some time, however, the issue in Britain will not be that of selective or non-selective education, but should comprehensive schools be neighbourhood schools with unbalanced intakes or should all such schools have the same ability spread; should such schools be banded or streamed or taught in all-ability groups; should there be open access to all courses in the schools by pupils and public; should there be a house system or a year system of pastoral care?

I do believe that at some stage some form of secondary school selection will have to return in Britain if our educational standards are to equal and preferably be superior to those in the rest of Europe. One point is certain. The return to selection will involve neither an 11-plus examination nor a bipartite arrangement. I would favour in urban areas specialist schools of all types, each having a basic curriculum and then 20 to 30 per cent of their time being allocated to their specialities. There could be mathematical schools, science schools, technical schools, craft schools, language schools, classical schools, sports schools. . . . Now we have the national curriculum it would be simple for pupils to change schools at almost any time during their secondary school career. I think such specialist schools would have better morale, with more interest from the pupils and the parents and, indeed, from employers. None of them would be sink schools, like we have in the centre of our cities at the present time, and all would have ambitious plans for increasing pupil morale.

If Mr Major allows the grant-maintained schools not only to increase in number but to have more control of their intake, the return of at least subject selection would arise naturally according to the market for schools in various areas. It is an interesting thought. Some form of selection will inevitably return.

The responsibility of parents is to find a school for their children which will give them the best education irrespective of what it is called or what type it is. I have been the head of a secondary modern school, a grammar school and a comprehensive school. I was a professional doing my job and I was proud at Highbury Grove to work with a governing body which was largely Labour, who worked with me because they (and their children) liked the way the school was run. That is professionalism. The responsibility of governors is to appoint the best headteachers and teachers possible and support them in their work. A good governing body is a great help to a headteacher and to a school.

6

The General Certificate of Education

As one who has always advocated external examinations for all pupils and pioneered them in my first headship in Lancashire, I was always suspicious (and still am) of one examination at the age of sixteen. One examination that can stretch the very able yet have meaning for the slowest pupils academically is practically an impossibility and it was to me an egalitarian instrument of levelling down invented by the educational establishment. What I always advocated were overlapping syllabuses so that pupils could easily move to whichever examination suited them at the age of sixteen.

When I was in charge of schools from 1981 to 1983 I advocated further GCE and 'O' level syllabus overlaps and a simple basic fifteen- or sixteen-year-old literacy and numeracy examination for the least able, which would indicate that the boy or girl was worth employing and had the basic skills. As an ex-secondary modern school teacher I considered and still consider this group to be the most deprived in British education because the education establishment pretends they do not exist or that they can improve their performance by the use of mirrors. For two years, while I was still in charge of schools, I attempted to slow down the movement to the single examination but unfortunately, before I had taken up this ministerial appointment, Mark Carlisle had already announced in February 1980 that 'the separate grading systems of GCE "O" levels and CSE must be incorporated in a single consistent system of clearly-defined goals, while the GCE "O" levels are retained'.

The General Certificate of Education

In 1986 the first pupils began the two-year course for the GCSE examination. There were new syllabuses, some of which would have fitted into *Gulliver's Travels*. Dear Sir Keith Joseph looked forward to fifth-form candidates having oral mathematical tests where they discussed the mathematical principles behind various forms of bridge building! The examination put itself at risk by having three different forms of examining and far too much course work, which always favours the pupil from the privileged home. Indeed, I said at the time that when the first GCSE certificates were presented in 1988, those that were largely on project methods should ask all the family to go up for their certificate and not just the ostensible student. As an historian I was also concerned about the degree of empathy expected from the pupils, particularly in history, where instead of learning historical facts and what life used to be like pupils had to try to imagine that they were characters in history and to write down their feelings at the time.

It is essential that the GCSE examination is shown to be fair and accurate and consistent from year to year. The fact that from the beginning there was a continued increase in the percentage passing at almost all grades threw early doubt on this. Indeed in 1988, the first year the GCSE was sat, 8.6 per cent of pupils passed at A grade as against only 6.8 per cent in the combined examinations of the previous year. One subject nearly doubled the number of A grades in a year. Over the following years there was a continued increase in the passes in the higher grades until 1995, when there was only a 1 per cent increase in the number of candidates gaining the top grades.

In the previous year, on 12 October 1994, there was a leading article in *The Times* concerning marking scripts in English from one of the most distinguished of the London schools. *The Times* article concluded: 'By appealing on behalf of its own pupils, Latymer may have performed an important national service. It has uncovered both individual mistakes and a larger mistaken philosophy. If schools are to be publicly accountable for their examination results, then the boards that hand out these results must also be open to scrutiny both for their procedure and their educational values.' In

1995 it seemed that the Boards took a firmer grip on examination marking and there was much less slippage. Overall the proportion graded A to C – which is supposed to be the old GCE standard – fell by 0.7 per cent in mathematics compared with 1988, while the English passes were up by 1.3 per cent.

Has the standard of children sitting the examination improved? This is possible since pupils are, I suspect, trying harder because of the tight employment situation and the difficulty of obtaining entry to our more distinguished universities, which are respected here and abroad. There is another factor: a change in the birth rate between various socio-economic groups. There is evidence that middle-class professional families are now having proportionally more children than the so-called lower classes. This is a trend that could bring a higher pass rate in its wake. This factor has been commented on by Professor Roger Murphy of Nottingham University.

There was one other factor regarding this year. Two of the Examining Boards were shown to be unduly lenient in 1994 and they were therefore compelled by the authorities that year to put in a set of common questions and also to carefully check the marking. There is a continued problem with tiering whereby in various subjects pupils are put into really separate examinations according to teacher decisions which limit what grades can be achieved. Mathematics has four separate tiers with teachers having the decision as to which standard the pupil should sit. English and geography are tiered, but history is untiered. The fact that there are different Boards could mean that these Boards, to increase their share of the total candidates, could lower their standards, but this would be self-destructive in the long run since good schools would enter their pupils for the stricter Boards.

Parents and governors know how important the GCSE examination is for the prospects of all children sitting. Governors must ensure that, with the co-operation of the headteachers, the best teachers are assigned to fifth-year classes as well as 'A' level classes and that every encouragement is given to such children to do well in their examinations. It is also vital that parents ensure that their children over this fifth school year are given every opportunity to maximize their academic abilities, particularly bearing in mind that the only examination grades that will be available when they apply for higher education courses will be those of the fifth-year GCSE.

7

'A' Levels, GNVQs and the Sixth-Form Curriculum

Examinations, like currency, must keep their value or they will lose credibility. The prestigious Joint Matriculation Board, based in Manchester, published reports as to how it made sure the standard of marking was the same every year. When I was in charge of schools at the Educational Department in 1982 I met Mr Vickerman, the Secretary of that Board, and asked him how they kept the standard the same every year at 'A' level. He told me of the infinite pains they went to, including markers having to re-mark scripts from various years to keep the standard static. Indeed I still have *Standards in GCE: Subject Passes Comparisons 1972–80*, published in 1982.

I then immediately sent a note to Sir Keith Joseph, the Secretary of State for Education, and copied it to other senior officials as follows:

SECRETARY OF STATE

I met Mr Vickerman, Secretary of the prestigious Joint Matriculation Board, yesterday afternoon with Mr Hedger. Mr Vickerman assures me that the Board attempt:

    i. to keep standards of marking and results equivalent over years and they keep samples of marked scripts back to 1952. This has bearing on the argument about state school standards;

    ii. to check with other Boards their marking levels;

    iii. to check that all subjects have equivalent marking.

2. It would seem to me that the Examinations Council will need

people like Mr Vickerman or otherwise we shall have to learn over the next 10 years what they have painfully learned over the last 30 years.

3. I also think it could be a good idea for you to meet Mr Vickerman if you can spare the time. I learned a good deal from him. I intend to visit him in Manchester to see the Board at work.

DR RHODES BOYSON
9th June 1982

c.c. Mr Ulrich, SCI, Mr Summers, Mr Hedger

There is thus no excuse for the five new examining boards not having kept full scripts over subsequent years. This is not the dog that did not bark but the dog that did not listen. The more people who sit 'A' level examinations the more important it is that the standard of marking is the same every year.

In 1950, the year before the Higher School Certificate became the Advanced Level, only 3 per cent of the age group sat and from my experience they were the *crème de la crème* academically. It was, however, decreed in 1951 that 30 per cent of 'A' level candidates should fail and be totally ungraded in their examinations. Since then more and more pupils have stayed on into the sixth form and sat 'A' levels and the Government has greatly increased the number of university and higher education places. More and more of these extra candidates must come from lower ability groups, yet apparently by magic or by special decree more and more pupils get more and more higher grades. The inflation in numbers and grades has increased each decade. In 1960 the fail rate at 'A' level had increased to 35 per cent. From then it fell to 23 per cent in 1990 to 16 per cent in 1994–5. In the same period of six years the number of A and B passes in the 'A' level examination increased by 22 per cent as a percentage of the overall passes. It seems now that, as in the Caucus Race, all must win prizes.

The Government, like an old Soviet state, also has 'targets' to increase these passes further. The Government aims to have 60 per cent of the age group having two 'A' levels by the year 2000. I previously had thought that this Government was a free market

Government where the market ruled and figures were real figures and not artificial projections which the Government then, by its influence, would make 'reality'! I do not believe that we are getting especially brainier year by year. I do accept that pupils in the struggle for good university places and future employment could be trying harder in the sixth form. I also accept that schools may be concentrating more on examination passes and league tables so that they can continue to recruit good pupils.

The integrity of the 'A' level examination is also put at risk by the six-week modules which pupils can study, have an examination at the end and sit again until they pass. This is a farce compared with pupils remembering facts and figures and arguments over two years, to write them up in the final 'A' level examination. The evidence is that mathematics and physics passes – where answers are right or wrong – have declined in numbers and grades over recent years. In 1965 a total of 38 per cent of 'A' level subject entries were in mathematics; now the percentage has dropped to only 9 per cent. There has been a 50 per cent drop in 'A' level mathematics entries since the 1980s despite a continued increase in the number of 'A' level candidates.

I think there is informal pressure on the one hand to pass more pupils and a slippage of marking standards on the other hand because of the number of poorer scripts which makes an average script look far better than it is. Originally only the very able sat; now pupils of average and lower ability sit and their very presence increases the marks to average and above-average candidates. The continued increase of the number of candidates and the number of higher grades being given will inevitably change the coinage and bring in, as at 'O' level, starred As for good candidates to simplify the university intake selection procedure, particularly for the very able.

John Redwood has stated that in 1993, as Welsh Secretary, he was concerned by the apparent decline of public examination standards and he asked to see marked scripts from a period of thirty years, but he was told he had no right to see them. In 1995, however, Mrs Gillian Shephard, the Secretary of State for Education and Employment, set up a study into the grading of 'A' level and

GCSE results in English, mathematics and science over the last twenty years. Many will wait for its conclusions with great interest.

Ironically, one area where it would seem that marking still has full integrity is in the area of the new General National Vocational Qualifications, started in 1992 as equivalent vocational qualifications to the academic 'A' levels. In 1995 only some 40 per cent of the 200,000 pupils taking these courses successfully completed them.

Sir Ron Dearing is at present conducting a review of the qualifications framework for sixteen- to nineteen-year-olds, having been given a personal remit by the Secretary of State for Education and Employment and the Secretary of State for Wales to maintain the rigour of GCSE 'A' levels; to continue to build on the current programmes for the development of the General National Vocational courses; to increase participation in achievement in education and training; to minimize wastage and to prepare young people for work and higher education, and to secure maximum value for money.

Labour has stated that it would change the 'A' levels, the Tory Reform Group wishes to phase 'A' levels out to be replaced by an examination of greater width rather than depth, and there is support for a five-subject course in the first-year sixth form, reducing to three subjects in the second-year sixth form. Any increase of breadth as against depth will be likely to necessitate a longer sixth-form course or a four-year degree course. The international baccalaureate has never taken off in Britain, while Scotland still has a five-subject certificate. Care must also be taken not to elongate courses for the GNVQ and NVQ examinations.

After sixteen years of Conservative Government I must add that I am concerned about the great increase in Government influence on examinations and education as a whole. The previous examination boards were independent academic bodies set up to preserve academic standards and independence. Now we have continued Government reports and an external examination system which is heavily influenced, if not totally controlled, by Government. I really do not think this is what sixteen years of Conservative Government was intended to achieve.

It is vital that parents and governors are aware of the various examinations available and what doors they can open. Pupils must make a careful choice of sixth-form subjects, bearing in mind their likely abilities and hopes of future employment. The more subjects there are and the more levels they can be taken at, the more essential it is that students are given correct advice, not only on their abilities but on how to achieve their future aims.

My own interim view is that the arrival and growth of the GNVQ at sixth-form level will entirely change the status of the sixth form. I am not convinced that media studies, photography, film studies, social work and health care are academic studies equivalent to 'A' levels, so it would seem to me that these studies should be under further education and not higher education. I would personally prefer the revival of apprenticeships with appropriate examinations on which the most able could go on to technical degrees at university. If the GNVQs really do not deliver the job prospects for those successfully sitting them there will be disappointment all round.

8

Apprenticeships

We need an educational system that produces both brain surgeons and plumbers. At the present time we are doing better with the brain surgeons than we are with the plumbers, since there seem to be fewer apprentices trained in Britain, and their training is often of a vagueness which does not equal the tightness of apprenticeship training on the Continent.

Until the Crowther Report of 1959 apprentices were expected to be accurate in their work and to complete the models that they were set to make according to the instructions of their teachers. The Crowther Report suggested, however, that apprentices should 'discover how things worked' and should have 'considerable theoretical knowledge'. Thus engineering drawing and metalwork became 'technology', moving away from accuracy and good finishing to non-structured experimentation.

Key Stage 4 (fourteen to sixteen years) of the national curriculum for technology is a vague amalgam of pupil aspirations far removed from the real world. Some fifty aims are listed, such as:

'design for manufacturing in quantity'
'to recognise that moral, economic, social, cultural and environmental issues make conflicting demands when designing'
'to devise and apply test procedures to check the quality of their work at critical points during the development and to indicate ways of improving it'

49

'to ensure that the quality of their products is suitable for intended users'

'taking responsibility for recognising hazards on products, activities and environments, including the unfamiliar'

I originally thought, until I looked at the national curriculum, that
these were spoofs and I have never seen a syllabus with so much
'mush'. It is no wonder that apprenticeship training is breaking down
in Britain. All that is missing in this part of the national curriculum
are references to 'apple pie' and 'motherhood'.

The training of apprentices in Germany, France, Holland and
Switzerland is very different from that in Britain. On the Continent
there is a tight curriculum taught together in relatively full classes,
and apprenticeship training starts earlier. The continental classes use
class teaching with all apprentices making the same object to a high
standard, such as key rings, metal boxes with metal hinges and tool
boxes. The teacher demonstrates on the Continent and the whole
class then works together. The teacher may stop the class to illustrate
a point from one student, but it will be a lesson for all the class.

British pupils, in contrast, often choose their own task, which
means there can be little or no class teaching and accuracy is therefore often sacrificed. The continental emphasis is on high quality,
clean working, reliability and punctuality and the motivation is higher.
There is rarely on the Continent the mixed project work with all
apprentices working at their own pace. In Britain apprentices make
model boats and aeroplanes, usually working at their own pace with
very little classroom structure or teaching.

On the Continent there is also much emphasis on practical drawing, which began to disappear in British schools some forty years
ago. The great difference is, however, that on the Continent apprentices do not waste time in problem-solving but concentrate on accuracy, reasonable speed and a good finish of the objects. Even when
in Britain a class of apprentices make a similar object pupils pro-
ceed at their own pace, which means no class teaching, the most
fruitful use of a teacher's time.

Pupils in Switzerland and Germany can leave school at fifteen and start their apprenticeships. In other countries the apprenticeship can be started at school in the pupil's early teens. I have always believed that we should let fifteen-year-olds leave school for apprenticeships provided they have passed a test in literacy and numeracy at the age of fifteen and have had a 95 per cent attendance in school in the year before leaving.

Switzerland trains its apprentices with great care for its excellent engineering industry. The accuracy of the work there of thirteen-year-olds hoping to be apprentices from the lower ability groups is generally well ahead of our sixteen-year-old apprentices. The Swiss apprenticeship training consists of making models according to age and ability and they are also expected to have a good grasp of mathematics. Similarly girls on the Continent sew, embroider and cook without wasting time on having to look up in encyclopaedias or the local library where the primary products come from and what sort of societies they live in.

In Holland there is strict specialization for fourteen- to sixteen-year-olds covering metalwork, electronics, motor vehicles, electrical engineering, office skills and catering. Sixty per cent of their time will be on their particular craft. Textbooks are used and there is full class teaching.

It really is time that we concentrated on apprentice teaching in Britain. As Professor Sig Prais of the National Institute for Economic and Social Research has indicated, there is likely to be a growing demand for more capable apprentices and journeymen. Professor Prais explains how the age of mechanization brought the replacement of skilled craftsmen by machines operated by unskilled or semi-skilled operatives. Now, however, in what he calls the age of automation, there is a growing demand for skilled men and women to manage the more sophisticated machinery which is beyond the understanding of unskilled school leavers. At present there are far more of these highly skilled craftsmen and women on the Continent than there are in Britain and unless action is taken this will limit Britain's economic prosperity.

Between 1983 and 1992 the number of apprentices in the building industry dropped from 18,000 to 2,000 in the London area. This is not only bad for industry, but also for Britain. With one-third of our male youths growing up in one-parent families, with no male model, they are now also deprived of the guidance they could gain from the journeyman who looks after them. It is thus no wonder that we have more male youngsters at war with society and each other to the severe disadvantage of our society.

Parents and governors should be aware of the drop in the number of those going on to train for skilled work and should ensure that there are good pre-apprenticeship courses leading to higher technical training introduced in all schools. Economic change and progress never stops and one has to think in employment terms of what is likely to be in demand in ten or twenty years' time.

Our greatest shortage in Britain is of technical graduates and technicians. Eighteen per cent of British youth are apprenticed as against 33 per cent in France, 56 per cent in Germany and 57 per cent in Sweden. Most of our apprentices qualify by serving their time, often without a written examination at the end. This is probably why we have so many breakdowns of the lifts and escalators on the London Underground. We have not yet learnt in Britain that there is going to be little employment for the under-achievers and a low standard of living for those without expertise.

9

Teacher Recruitment and Training

My mother had always wanted to be a teacher and as the youngest of a family of fourteen children she had been promised the grammar school. At the last moment, however, my grandfather – a Lancashire hill farmer – changed his mind and sent her to the mill as a half-timer. She was broken-hearted and cried in her bed every night for months. Not until she was thirty-nine, when I was born, was she released from the slavery of the mill. I was thus a double blessing: she wanted a child and she also wanted to be out of the mill, and no self-respecting nonconformist would, under the conventions of that time, allow his wife to work once she had a child to bring up. It was alleged that in certain bedrooms in Lancashire the motto over the bed was not the religious slogan *Prepare to meet thy doom*, but the even more bitter *Prepare to meet thy loom*. A child for many a Lancashire mother meant the blessed release from the factory whistle and the clattering weaving-shed.

My mother always wanted me to be a teacher and my father was a giant of the early Labour and trade union movement where books and culture were esteemed above riches and he was an expert in self-education all his life, teaching himself Esperanto and other languages and politics and philosophy. I inherited from him a library of nearly a thousand books made up of the classics, socialist and communist works and the Left and Right Book Clubs of the 1930s.

When I returned from the Royal Navy in 1947 schoolmastering was still a very respected profession in Lancashire. In the 1930s and 1940s the grammar school teacher and the elementary school

53

headmaster could afford to run a car and they had a pensionable job and middle-class girls and able working-class boys were easily recruited into teaching.

Economically, as compared with other occupations, teaching has gone down-market at the same time as teachers are sadly less respected. Teachers in the 1950s were recruited from the two-year teacher training colleges at the age of nineteen or twenty. They largely taught in the primary schools and in the secondary modern schools. Those who took degrees then took a one-year teacher training course and taught in the secondary modern and grammar schools.

There was, however, an anomaly that all people with degrees could teach without a need for a professional training certificate. Many such graduates thus tried teaching and, with or without a teaching degree qualification, taught for the rest of their lives. We have lost many good graduates by the restriction on this entry, which was basically brought in to buy peace with the teacher unions and to make teaching an all-graduate profession for status purposes.

I suspect we had a better level of teacher recruitment when we had a two-year teacher qualification as against today's three-year and four-year courses. This is because lively and intelligent girls took the two-year course as an insurance against future unemployment or the death of a husband and then found that they liked teaching and stayed in the profession. No way, however, are such girls likely to take a four-year course for a teaching future they are uncertain about.

How can we train teachers? Some really need no training and are born teachers and they are the greatest gift to the teaching profession. A far larger body of young men and women can, over a period of time, learn the techniques of teaching. Alas, some potential teacher recruits have so little personality that they will never enthuse a class to the excitement of learning.

I have always considered that the best training for teachers is the real school situation. I learnt more in my two school practices than I did in any lectures, with the exception of those given by my tutor who was an expert in the education of young children. I think a year in the classroom, alongside a gifted teacher who is paid for his or her additional responsibilities, is worth all the lectures in existence.

The best teachers as a body I have ever met were the emergency-trained teachers after World War II. They were largely ex-servicemen and women who had, in many cases, long service experience and were trained on thirteen-month courses by existing heads and deputy heads seconded from their schools. They were taught all the tricks of teaching and quickly became highly proficient, and I was fortunate to have one of their products as my supervising teacher in my first teaching practice. It was the emergency-trained teachers who carried the raising of the school-leaving age soon after World War II, since their worldly experience was respected by the pupils who otherwise resented the extra year at school. We lacked such mature individuals when we raised the school-leaving age to sixteen in 1973 – my last year as a headmaster.

The second best set of teachers I ever met were the pupil-teacher trained teachers who qualified in the early years of this century. They were trained in the schools they attended, receiving tuition from the staff as they gained their teaching qualifications. They too knew all the tricks of the trade and were honed at the blackboard.

Amongst the mature staff at Highbury Grove I had the best remedial teacher I have ever met and I used to put young teachers in his Department to learn for a week what teachers could achieve. He and his pupils were present willingly and voluntarily from 8 a.m. in the morning to at least 6 p.m. in the evening.

There is still a suspicion that teacher training institutions not only spend too much time on outlandish schemes, but that some are filled with the addicts of political correctness and left-wing dogma. *The Times* in a leader in March 1995 stated, 'Their image as Marxist-dominated havens of failed teaching methods may be sometimes exaggerated: but there is little doubt that the colleges have encouraged some of the discredited practices that ministers are trying to sweep away. Students' own accounts of courses divorced from the reality of school life encouraged the belief that some current trends contribute more to the problems of the education service than to their solutions.'

We have the evidence against one teacher training college where a well-qualified applicant was rejected without interview when she applied in her own name – white and British – but was invited for interview when she applied under an assumed name with a letter of application badly punctuated and misspelt, but stating that her special interests were anti-blood sports and the Animal Liberation Front. In 1993 a student won a legal case against the Secretary of State for Scotland arguing that the course was so dominated by left-wing theory that it did not constitute proper training. The *Sunday Telegraph* commented on this case on 18 April 1993, 'The course . . . has turned out to be largely left-wing sociology overlaid with Politically Correct discipline.'

The overall degree standards of those recruited for teaching is low. In 1994 more than 27 per cent of those expecting to attain third-class honours planned to go into teaching, as against 9 per cent of those expecting first-class honours degrees. Perhaps there should be bonuses for teachers with first- and second-class honours degrees. This reminds me that one of my first actions when I was in charge of higher education in 1979 was to ensure that no one could be recruited for teacher training without 'O' levels in English and mathematics. Previously 37 per cent of those recruited for teachers training had not 'O' level mathematics and 5 per cent had not even 'O' level English! It was only in 1995 that the Government laid down that every teacher recruit had to have one science subject at GCSE!

Status, partially at least, comes from relative income levels and teaching has done badly in recent years. Between 1972 and 1990 the real income of nurses increased by 62 per cent as against 13 per cent for teachers. At the same time teaching has become more demanding and stressful, with national tests on one side and the withdrawal of the sanction of corporal punishment on the other. There is a shortage of good teacher applicants, especially in mathematics, science, design and technology and languages. In 1995 there was a 10 per cent drop in teacher trainee applicants who read mathematics and an even greater drop in teacher trainee applicants who had read science and modern languages. At the same time more teachers are resigning before their retirement age. Thirty per cent of headmasters are now resigning before their time and since 1988 there has also been a 20 per cent decline in applications for headships and a 30 per cent decline in applications for deputy headships.

Teaching has also never really recovered from the withdrawal of so many of the profession from professional, as against statutory, duties some years ago. Indeed, when I was an Education Minister I fought hard and prevented the introduction of the 1,265-hour yearly contract, which to my mind is the end of a profession. A professional person finishes the job in as many hours as it takes, rather than watching the clock. I never timed my staff to a set number of hours. I expected them to be present when required and for me to give them full leave when they requested it.

I really do not think that a National Vocational Qualification Level 5 as a preparation for headship will raise the sights of my erstwhile profession. Far better to set up on the lines of the armed service colleges a headmasters' staff college where the most capable heads are trained. It is vital that the status of the profession is raised. Why not take over the Royal Naval College, Greenwich, as this new headmasters' staff college? This might also remind heads of the rich maritime history of our country.

Teachers need the support of governors and parents if a school is to be successful. The post of chairman or chairlady of a grant-maintained school or one under local financial management is very responsible and the governors should be careful who they choose. Let me, however, give one piece of advice. Interviews are probably the most ineffective method of appointing teaching staff. I can well remember the appointment of a head of drama in one of my schools. One applicant gave a most dramatic interview but, alas, that was the only drama that was in him and within a term I had to dismiss him. Nobody would buy a 'soccer player' at an interview. Instead the player would be watched in a game. The only way to know whether a teacher is fully effective is for a competent individual to see him not at an interview but actually teaching at the blackboard.

10

Religious, Moral and Sex Education

Schools are not neutral institutions to train clever devils. They exist to prepare the young for adulthood by passing on the values as well as the skills of our society. Honesty is to be commended and cruelty is evil. Moral codes are concerned with what life is about, which is linked for most of us with our views on religion. This does not mean that the atheist has no morality. Indeed, many an atheist with no belief in an immortal soul can be highly respected for his personal moral code.

The 1944 Education Act was passed at a time when the evil creed of Nazism had brought low a great nation, Germany. There was overwhelming support in Parliament for the religious clauses in this Act, which laid down that each school day should start with an act of 'collective worship' and that there should be religious education classes for all children whose parents did not specifically object.

One can indeed argue that no one can understand the society in which we live without a full understanding of Christianity, which has affected all our values. This applies to out literature, our art, our music and even our calendar. The architects of the 1944 Education Act desired healthy minds in healthy bodies and religious education and physical education were, in certain authorities, the only subjects that were specifically compulsory. It could be said that religion was the fourth 'R' with reading, writing and arithmetic!

Religion has, however, gone through a number of crises in the last fifty years, especially among its clerical leaders. Attendance at church has declined, although more go to church on Sundays than

58

watch soccer on Saturdays, and *Songs of Praise* on television has a huge and faithful audience. It is largely the pseudo-intellectuals who have left religion. As always there is also the treason of the clerks.

Surveys indicate that 65 to 70 per cent of our people consider themselves to be Christians and would like their children taught Christianity in schools. Although the religious education syllabus now gives 30 per cent of its time to religions other than Christianity, only 1.9 per cent of parents register in schools as members of other religions.

We have, of course, Jewish schools for Jewish children funded almost fully by the State and I consider that the Government has been very remiss in not accepting the full funding of Muslim schools which fulfil the national curriculum and also have fully trained teachers. This is especially the case in Yusuf Islam's school in Brent. We also now have in Brent the first Hindu school, which similarly has qualified teachers and covers the national curriculum. The claim that we are now a multi-racial and multi-cultural society and schools should be totally secular does not hold water. Religion is part of our society and the immigrant community expects schools to have a moral message.

I find it amazing that the churches have not ensured that the religious clauses of the 1944 Act are fully enforced. Why have the churches not trained special teachers to teach religious education in schools and to volunteer to take morning school assemblies? I was surprised when I was an education minister to visit one religious training college where far more were studying sociology than religion. A communist once said to me that if they had then been allowed to have a communist assembly in every school every day and two lessons of communism each week in the classroom they could have won the general election! I doubt that, but he certainly has a point.

I suspect that religious education is only half-heartedly taught in many schools. Solzhenitsyn refers to 'societies where the defence reactions have been paralysed'. C. S. Lewis wrote that if we are aiming for Heaven we could get Earth thrown in, but if we merely aimed at Earth we would get neither.

The 1988 Education Act reinforced the Government's support for collective worship and religious education in schools. Dr Nick Tate, the Chief Inspector of the Schools Council Curriculum and Assessment Authority, stated in 1993 that half our schools were breaking the law on religious education and that Britain was 'far advanced in becoming a religious illiterate society'. He also announced a new religious education syllabus for fourteen- to sixteen-year-olds which would count as half a GCSE. The 1992 Education Act ensured that religious education was inspected alongside other subjects and there seems to have been a revival in this subject with an increase in the numbers sitting it as a GCSE subject in recent years.

I took morning assembly every day in my schools when I was a headteacher. As a Christian believer I considered the hymns, prayers and readings to be very important. I always said, however, at the beginning of the school year at the first assembly that I was a Christian believer but many staff and pupils were not, but I welcomed them all to assembly because Christianity was part of our society, and without it we would not understand its values. I never proselytized. Practically all staff attended such assemblies every day. I sometimes suspect that the retreat from the full school morning assembly in large schools is because some headteachers cannot get silence from 1,250 pupils. A headteacher who can get such silence is in charge of his school and his staff and the boys and girls know he is in charge. A good assembly starts a good day. The non-religious part of the morning assembly, informing all pupils of sports achievements and other activities, also puts a unity on a school. Morning assembly should be short, cheerful, inspiring and, at times, hilarious. Laughter is a badge of belonging.

It was because I never preached as such in assembly that I had no problems with full attendance. When I was the Headmaster of the Robert Montefiore School in the East End of London I had Jewish, Christian and Muslim children. I contacted the leaders of the three communities and we agreed on ten hymns which we could all sing and a number of prayers that I could use, which mentioned God but not Jesus. Before long we knew these prayers, readings and hymns by heart.

Religious, Moral and Sex Education

When I was Headmaster of Highbury Grove School we had a number of Jewish boys who attended assembly and some thirty Catholic boys. I arranged for a Catholic priest to say Mass one morning a week with these boys and on the other four mornings they attended my assembly. I did not report this to my governors, but I am sure they would have approved if I had done so. A little private enterprise goes well in any institution.

The 1987 *Reader's Digest* survey showed overwhelmingly that parents wanted their children taught the difference between right and wrong, though support specifically for religious education was less overwhelming. I suspect, however, that almost all parents would support the teaching of the Ten Commandments as the basis of the good life, despite the fact that so many now fall below their full execution in their own lives.

I consider that sex education is a definite moral area and is not a branch of athletics. Sex education is thus best given by a mature parent or close relative who knows the boy or girl very well and if this cannot be done at home then a housemaster or a senior member of staff could be asked to perform the necessary task of information-giving. I have always supported the right of parents to withdraw their children from any form of sex education in school and I am glad that this has now been guaranteed in legislation. All sex has moral connotations and children mature differently so if such education is given to a whole class some would take it in their stride while others – possibly not as mature – would find it mentally disturbing. There is a mental age in this matter as well as a physical age and there is no way that a whole class can be at the same point of development.

Let me make two other points. I found when sex education was discussed at staff meetings that the ones who wished to teach it were the ones with most hang-ups in this particular area, while the ones leading what one would consider a normal life had little enthusiasm to teach it. Secondly, in an age which still has much of the 'discovery method' in it, if one teaches sex education in a class then some of them will go out and 'discover' it. I do not think it is accidental that the rise of illegitimate births and the increase of sex among those under sixteen has coincided with the increased teaching of sex education in schools.

I do not think that the issue of single or mixed schools is a moral matter, though some strict Muslim parents could disagree with me and their views should certainly be taken into account. The judgement on single or mixed schools should be simply on which type of school is most efficient educationally. The social side of life is important, but school is only part of life and schools are basically for teaching. The first school in which I taught was mixed, as were those of my first two headships. I then became Headmaster of Highbury Grove, a tough, sporting boys' school of 1,250 healthy males. I realized on my first day of morning assembly that a boys' school was easier to run than a mixed school. In assembly one spoke to the interests of boys and there was only one audience. In a mixed school there are two audiences – girls and boys with different interests. I then came to the conclusion that the only real advantages of mixed education were that boys became slightly less boisterous; that the presence of girls makes casting of plays easier and that while girls usually revolt in the third year of secondary school boys revolt in the fourth year so one has only half the class in revolt at any time! In any case boys are pack animals while girls are individuals.

In the state sector grammar schools, except in rural areas, were generally single sex and I remember when I came to London to the Robert Montefiore School, the fact that it was mixed surprised people because they presumed that all academic schools must be single sex. Then we had the move to the comprehensive school and over the last thirty years the number of single-sex secondary state schools dropped from 2,500 to 300, while the pupils sampled the delights of co-education. This change took place with no research and no questioning of parents. It was the political correctness of its time!

Until recently public schools were overwhelmingly single sex; then, presumably again for political correctness and also to poach very bright girls from girls' schools, many of the boys' public schools started recruiting sixth-form girls and even pupils of younger age. Of the 240 HMC schools, 135 are now fully co-educational or recruiting girls in the sixth form. Now we know from the league tables that the best academic results overall are from single-sex schools. In 1994 only two of the top fifty schools in the league tables were mixed. The rest were single sex. In 1995 fifteen of the twenty best public schools and thirty-five of the top fifty public schools in the league tables were single sex. Similarly the highest achieving state schools in the league tables were single sex. It would appear to me that parents in urban areas should now have a choice of single-sex or co-educational education. In the state sector the change to co-educational schools was simply a fashion and local education authorities should be directed – if we are concerned for academic standards in our country – to give parents a choice of single or co-educational schools once again. With pupils maturing sexually at an earlier age the separation of the sexes could be more important in the secondary school, otherwise the presence of an attractive girl may easily be more powerful than the beauty of an Elizabethan sonnet.

I suspect that one of the reasons that girls are now out-pacing boys in their educational achievements at all levels is that there has been a weakening of discipline in many schools, which causes boys to suffer more than girls since girls are much more likely to work successfully on their own while most boys only reach their potential in a tightly disciplined environment.

The ethical, moral and religious background of a school should always be checked by parents and governors. To many parents this quite rightly is a most important factor in their choice of school.

11

School Discipline

'Discipline' in the years of revolt between the late 1960s and the early 1970s became a word associated with the whip and the jackboot. Discipline, however, originally meant instruction from a teacher to his disciples and scholars, which I still believe is what education is about, and without such a relationship allowing the teachers to teach and the disciples to learn schools will have no proper ethos. Boys like discipline if it is fair and they then thrive on it. When I came to London in 1961 many schools claimed to be the one where a boy was held by his braces outside a classroom window four storeys up!

A school should be a purposeful, cheerful community, with the teachers in charge, and the more that the staff and the pupils identify with its aims the better the school will be. The job of the headteacher and the teaching staff is to create the right relationship. There must be a shared confidence, a sense of community, pride, sense of values and, at its best, a joint sense of humour.

Every school must have something of which all its members are proud. At Highbury Grove, my last school, it was soccer, a learning situation, the attentions of the media, and the school that had the most badges. We were near the famous Arsenal soccer ground and we had ten or more soccer teams turning out every Saturday morning and they usually won. When Arsenal was playing at home in a cup tie, without any communication with the Inner London Education Authority, I changed the school hours to 8 a.m. to 1 p.m. so that pupils and staff could attend the match and on such days the boys wore their Arsenal scarves with their school uniform. I remember boy after boy replying when I interviewed them for entry that the reason they wished to come to Highbury was 'for soccer, sir'. One boy surprisingly said he wished to come 'because I hear that I can build a spacecraft here'. He was in: a boy with ambition!

The media arrived by geography. Islington is full of media people and if they wanted an educational story Highbury Grove could always oblige. The media also sent their sons to Highbury Grove, after they checked academic results, and I am rather sorry that it is over twenty years since I was there, otherwise Mr Blair could have opted to send his son to Highbury Grove without getting into trouble with his left-wingers.

The badges were designed within the school and extra badges could be won for all kinds of achievement. Boys love badges and we had so many at Highbury Grove that they slowed the boys down when they wanted to rush round the school!

A school has to deliver a good education which is respected by the parents. The staff have also to feel they are important. When Highbury Grove opened I watched one member of staff who looked as if he would be difficult. Then one day he stopped me in a corridor and said, 'You have won – someone yesterday told my wife on a train how lucky I was to teach here.' The wives and husbands of staff must always be treated royally. No man or woman will work more than their partner lets them. There must be regular get-togethers and staff must be introduced to visiting notabilities.

Parental commitment is also critical. This too can boost order inside a school. We had six houses at Highbury Grove and six parental associations and regular house assemblies. Every evening the school was filled with parents and boys in the house associations in an intense social and sporting life. The great battle to appoint my deputy headmaster as the next Head when I left the school in 1974 was led from the house associations who literally locked out the interviewing committee and candidates from the Inner London Education Authority and eventually, after many months, got the man they wanted. Commitment to Highbury Grove for all of us preceded any politics and on the eighteen-strong governing body only two were Conservative; the majority were working-class Labour with one or two Fabians that I had to keep an eye on.

Despite all this activity there were occasional disciplinary problems. When the school opened, the fourth-year pupils from the secondary modern school and from the residual school who intended leaving at the end of that year showed no enthusiasm for being 'privileged' to attend Highbury Grove and I realized that at the first autumn half-term something had to be done. This is where the badges came in. I decided to make all the fourth-year leavers lance corporals. Accordingly a list of daily duties was prepared for some forty boys and since one house was on duty one day in six, responsibilities were thus found for all fourth-year boys leaving that year. Large marshal and deputy-marshal badges were produced in ornate house colours and issued to fourth-year boys by me on the day school returned from the October half-term break. Gates were given names from the humdrum to the exotic – Dustbin Alley, Headmaster's Gate, Chelsea Gate, Chittagong Gate, China Gate – and boys were told of their responsibilities to ensure that there was good behaviour near them and no boy slipped out at morning break to the tempting world outside.

The fourth-year boys were transformed. They now belonged and had specific responsibilities. Not only did the duty house fourth-former stand by his gate and post, but boys from the other five houses who were allocated on the other days to that gate also stood alongside to ensure that all was well. Every day I went round with the duty housemaster to speak to the boys on duty and all became sweetness and light.

A sense of humour is always an advantage, particularly if it is shared by a school. I always said to the boys that it is their job to revolt and mine to put them down, but they must never win otherwise the game was over. I grew my side whiskers after a humorous agreement with the sixth form that they would cut their long hair (which was kept clean but irritated the housemasters) if I grew my side whiskers. This we agreed and I have had my side whiskers ever since as a memento of Highbury Grove.

It is very important for each boy (or girl) to feel that they are privileged to be a member of the school. If there are 250 vacancies one year and only 249 applications then morale will slump. With 251 applications every boy can feel that he is privileged to be in the school and that the school is a guards division or a regiment of the line and not the equivalent of the pioneer corps.

I still think that overall the withdrawal of corporal punishment in 1984 has made the task of teachers, particularly amongst boys in secondary schools, more difficult. Corporal punishment certainly does not solve all problems, but the knowledge that it exists in the school and is used where necessary was certainly a constraint on pupil misbehaviour. Sadly nothing else has been put in its place by Government. The fact also that parents in certain schools will not let their children stay in detention is not a help to an ordered community. I certainly have sympathy with the many teachers struggling for class control these days. The withdrawal of corporal punishment also means a weakening of the close relationship between pupils and staff. No longer are the staff *pro parentis* as in the past and the teachers have become more like detached instructors, since the teacher is no longer a person of such authority. Mrs Shephard, the Secretary of State for Education and Employment, stated in the autumn of 1995 that she was considering extending the powers of headteachers in the detention and expulsion of pupils.

The classroom teacher must be in charge of the class. He must be present before the children arrive, have his lesson ready and set work which is challenging but within the grasp of the class. I still prefer rows of desks with younger children, where there is less chattering and where one can see clearly where each pupil always is. All books should be regularly marked, especially homework books. Every lesson, however, should have some fun or excitement. Children like healthy humour and they like their teacher to be a 'character' about whom they can boast to other pupils and to their family at home. Beware, however, of snide or cynical comments about pupils.

It is estimated that 500,000 pupils, 10 per cent of the school population, are absent every day with some 100,000 rarely or never in attendance. In many cases the classroom teachers would prefer them absent so that there is less disruption and the teacher can teach those who want to learn. The 100,000 are probably a lost generation.

I believe that it was a mistake to rename school attendance officers as education welfare officers. Titles matter and school attendance is the job of school attendance officers. Once they became education welfare officers they tried to become amateur psychologists instead of frog-marching children back into school. I believe that each secondary school should have a school attendance officer who is also responsible for the feed primary schools. Since we have league tables for examinations now, why not have league tables published for every school for attendance, since education only starts when the pupil comes inside the classroom and sits at his or her desk! Indeed, the salary of each school attendance officer can be directly linked with the percentage attendance in the school. I have no doubt that if one did link salaries with the percentage of school attendance there would be an immediate improvement. These league tables must just show the percentage absent irrespective of the reason otherwise they would be useless. Inspectors visiting schools must check the registers against the names of the pupils as they did in the 1930s. Truancy matters not just because the pupils are losing education but because if they spend the last one, two or three years of their schooling as truants they develop a way of life at war with society and can easily slip into a life of criminality.

Over the eight years at Highbury Grove I took in a number of problem boys from other schools and they fitted into our disciplinary arrangements. I suspended only one boy and this was for a vicious attack on a master. I was then put under pressure to bring him back into the school, which I refused. I was then persuaded that there would have to be a full conference in the school about him and I went over with the boy's housemaster to one of the house rooms, where there were numerous officials, school attendance officers, psychologists, social workers . . . all sitting round with the boy and his parents in attendance. The Chairman started the meeting by saying we were all guilty. He got no further, since I stood up and said to my housemaster, 'Since you and I are not guilty at all we are in the wrong meeting', and we left the meeting. It was never reconvened, nor did the boy come back to my school.

It is very difficult to compare discipline in one decade to another.

There seems, however, more stress in many areas of teaching now. In 1987 the Professional Association of Teachers estimated that one-third of its members had been physically attacked in school; the *Sunday Times* in 1993 estimated that something like 16,000 teachers were assaulted each year and the National Association of Schoolmasters/Union of Women Teachers, led by its General Secretary Nigel de Gruchy, stated in 1995 that pupil violence was increasing. The National Association of Head Teachers had sixty-nine cases of verbal or physical abuse reported to them in 1995 and was handling twelve criminal compensation cases. The number of cases was thirty-seven up on 1994. The number of permanent pupil exclusions has risen from 2910 in 1990–91 to 11,811 in 1993–4.

The murder in 1995 of Philip Lawrence, the Headmaster of St George's School in Maida Vale, may have been outside the school gates, but it was an indication of the increasing dangers to life and limb in the school situation.

Parents and governors should give full support to headteachers and teachers in maintaining good discipline in schools. Without good discipline there will be no real education. Parents should sign a pledge that they will support the school in insisting on regular attendance and good behaviour, and firm action should be taken against any parent who refuses to sign such a commitment.

My own view is that teaching has become a much more stressful occupation. The recent figure that only one in six teachers now continue to the normal retiring age is, if it is correct, a very sad commentary on our age.

12

Sports Education

It is doubtful whether the Duke of Wellington ever declared, 'The Battle of Waterloo was won on the playing fields of Eton', but there has been a long-term view in our country that sport is useful in increasing fitness, giving a sense of fair play and helping people to be part of a team. Since the time of the ancient Greeks sport has been part of the education of the whole man.

I was fortunate to be born in a small Lancashire village at a time of little traffic with no worry about small children playing in the street. Life was safer and freer. Every day after school we put down our jackets and played soccer and cricket with whatever balls and pieces of wood were available. At the grammar school I was proud to play for my house and my school and for the local Air Training Corps. Sport was part of almost all our lives. On Saturday afternoons we watched Haslingden play cricket in the prestigious Lancashire League. When I became a schoolmaster I immediately looked after a team and when I became a headmaster I regularly watched Saturday school matches. At school I enjoyed swimming, but I was never keen on gymnastics. We now have a new age, however, with the one-eyed videos and the multiple television channels jockeying for position. The effect on the health of the nation must in the long run be very serious.

British schools, particularly the public schools and the grammar schools, had much sport as part of the curriculum. Again following the Greek ideal, this was very different from most European schools which have little or no sport. The decline of school sport in Britain is much to be deplored. Sport in school time has also declined under the pressure of the national curriculum, the withdrawal of teachers from voluntary activities in 1985, the stress on the 1,265 hours a year teaching contract, which I objected to when I was an Education Minister because it was the end of a profession. It was brought in by Sir Keith Joseph soon after I left the Department. We also have the demands of working wives that their husbands should help them with the shopping on Saturday morning instead of looking after a school team.

The number of physical education teachers in schools has declined by some 20–25 per cent since the national curriculum was introduced. Physical education departments are expensive and are subject to cuts to keep up expenditure in other departments. Many physical education colleges have closed and there are very few trained physical education teachers now in our primary schools.

Perhaps we will need the threat of a land war to bring school physical education up to scratch again. As in everything, education goes in circles and the sight of huge numbers of overweight children in our schools could change the attitude of the Government, bringing physical education back into favour. However, the grants from the National Lottery to promote physical education will be farcically small compared with the cuts that have already been made.

A secondary heads' survey in 1995 indicated that three out of four schools were now giving less time for sport. The decline is largest in the State sector; independent schools generally give 50 per cent more time to such activities. Most team games were invented by London apprentices and codified in Victorian schools and universities. Perhaps in this spectator age they can only be saved by the creation of super sports schools as part of a return to secondary school specialization. Such schools would certainly improve our international sporting performances.

I still think that up to the age of sixteen, two hours of physical education a week should be compulsory for all but the genuine conscientious objectors. This adds up to one lesson of gymnastics, one lesson of swimming and one hour of games a week. I think for safety reasons all children should be able to swim by the age of eleven. Unfortunately, there seems a decline in the willingness of parents to assist with school games.

Early in the 1970s, as one of the regular educational nonsenses, there came a move by the colleges of education towards individual activities – as against competitive sport, which was then considered a part of the capitalist society to be resisted. At that stage I interviewed a newly-qualified teacher who objected to teaching all team games. Presumably if he was fit enough yet played *slow* table tennis his right hand could play his left without putting at risk his socialist idealism; I should imagine in his case the left hand would win.

Far more dangerous in the long run has been the selling off of playing-fields since 1979 to raise local capital finance. This was not only a mistake in sporting terms, but it was bad town planning since sports fields are the lungs of an area and what people want is not a green belt fifty miles away at the end of a motorway, but some green playing-fields five or ten minutes' walk from their homes.

I am still old-fashioned enough to believe that well-supervised games teach fitness, the ability to withstand pressures and to know oneself. Highbury Grove School was, of course, near the Arsenal and it revolved round soccer and boys opted for the school because of this. At their interviews boys would mention that they wished to come to Highbury Grove because of the number of soccer teams that we put out in every week. Parents have shown, as in the 1987 *Reader's Digest* survey, that they want their children to continue to have competitive sport. As almost always, the man and woman in the street has more sense than the so-called experts.

I would make two further points. The first is that I have spoken of boys' sports, since these were the ones I followed and my last school was just boys. In my previous mixed schools I did watch netball and rounders and other girls' games. My last comment is that in my twenty-three years of schoolmastering I did meet a few boys and possibly more girls to whom competitive sport was an anathema. I accepted this and found them something else to do. Children similarly accept the differences of their schoolmates.

Parents and governors must, for the sake of our present and future generations, fight for the retention of playing-fields and competitive sport, otherwise children and young people will be deprived of games, which are not only enjoyable but do a great deal for the continued physical fitness of our people. Playing-fields built over are destroyed for all time. Governors can also encourage parents to take responsibility under the headteacher for certain physical games and activities as part of their public service, provided they are regularly reminded that games are games to be played under proper rules and in the right spirit and not just for personal or school satisfaction. The game must always be greater than the prize.

13

Assisted Places, Grant-maintained Schools and the Educational Voucher

Two successes of the Conservative Government have been the assisted places scheme and the grant-maintained school. The Labour Government of 1974–9 destroyed the direct grant schools because they were on one side selective and on the other side fee-paying by most of the pupils. Thus indirectly public funds subsidized not only needy working-class children but also children from affluent homes.

The Labour Party gave the direct grant schools the choice of becoming non-fee-paying and comprehensive in their intake or of going totally independent. Most of them went independent on academic grounds, while a number of the Catholic direct grant schools came into the State sector. The Labour Party over these five years was probably the greatest creator of independent schools since the Middle Ages!

In opposition between 1974 and 1979 the Conservative Party discussed what could be done to open these direct grant schools again to pupils from low-income homes, and we came up with a scheme which I believe is a much better scheme than the direct grant scheme. We decided to subsidize the pupils directly and not the schools. Pupils from low income homes are subsidized according to their parents' incomes when they are accepted into the ex-direct grant schools. I had envisaged some 15,000 a year being so subsidized, but the Education Department, wedded to the comprehensive system, fought against this number and I had finally to settle for 5,500 children a year.

The scheme has been highly successful. There are five candidates for every vacant place. The income level has allowed 30 per cent of pupils to be totally free, 43 per cent of pupils to receive some help and some 27 per cent who applied originally for direct grant places finish up paying the fees from various sources.

It is true that some middle-class families, such as those of vicars, teachers and divorced mothers are subsidized, but I am now convinced that the pupils come from a wide variety of homes. There are children of bus drivers, agricultural workers, postal workers, nurses, milkmen and the unemployed. King Edward VI School in Birmingham has 110 assisted places, half of them from homes with an income of less than £9,000 a year. The average income of all families on assisted places last year was only £10,975. The total cost was £104 million. In areas like Bradford many of the recipients came from first- and second-generation Asian immigrant families. One-fifth of assisted-place pupils come from the top socio-economic group, AB; two-fifths come from the middle classes, C1; one-fifth from the skilled working class, C2; and one-fifth from the lower social group, D.

Most of the direct grant schools came back into the scheme and there is a waiting list of other independent schools which would like to join. Most independent school teachers welcome the opportunity of teaching bright children from whatever background they come. I now consider the scheme one of the best methods of reverse discrimination ever introduced in Britain and I find it amazing that the Labour and Liberal-Democrat parties, blinded by their opposition to any form of selection, still oppose it.

I remember one Sunday afternoon knocking on doors in my constituency, as is my habit. It was a council housing estate. Suddenly a whole family rushed out to greet me. There was mother and father and two boys, both of whom were on the Assisted Places Scheme, and I had the greatest difficulty in getting away from that family because of their enthusiasm for the scheme, but it was a day I was proud to be in politics. A Mori poll commissioned by ISIS in 1994 showed that three out of five Labour supporters favoured the scheme.

The Prime Minister has pledged to double the number of assisted places and to extend the scheme to ages below eleven. This statement of extending the scheme to junior departments of independent schools was welcomed by the schools themselves.

I have always believed that schools should be answerable to parents and not to education authorities. The only people who are totally committed to the interests of a pupil are the parents and they probably know their children better than anybody else. Another argument for parent power is that if the home and the school are in full agreement then pupils will be much more likely to reach their full potential. Indeed, I always said when I was appointed to a headship that if in any year there were less applicants wanting to join my school than there were places available I would resign on the spot. This was not a vain boast, since two of the three schools to whose headship I was appointed had more vacancies than pupils the year before my appointment.

I have thus totally supported the grant-maintained school since its introduction. This makes the school totally independent of the local authority and under local parental control. I was not surprised that the Labour Party at that time opposed it, since the Labour Party has always felt that the man or woman at County Hall knows best.

The 1988 Education Reform Act brought in the grant-maintained school. Parents have to vote such a school into existence. The first secondary school joined in 1989 and the first primary school came in two years later. There are at least fifteen locally elected and co-opted governors on each of their governing bodies, many of them parents and teachers.

In my constituency of Brent North all but one of my secondary schools – including a Roman Catholic one – are grant-maintained. Over the country there are now some 625 secondary grant-maintained schools and some 415 primary grant-maintained schools. About one-fifth of secondary schools in England and Wales are now grant-maintained. Twice as many parental ballots have been won as have been lost to become grant-maintained. However, only 2 per cent of Catholic schools and 4 per cent of Anglican schools have become grant-maintained.

The first advantage of a grant-maintained school is that it will receive 100 per cent funding from the Government as against the

10–15 per cent that is kept back by local authorities. The second advantage is that the school is virtually independent despite being funded by Government. The third advantage is that there has been a more liberal distribution of Government building funds to grant-maintained schools than to non-grant-maintained schools.

The disadvantages of grant-maintained schools are that the schools cannot rely on local government support if they have serious problems. They would have to buy advice. Another disadvantage is that the grant-maintained school could be a stepping-stone to total Government control since all its money comes from Government, and should there be a left-wing socialist Government such schools would be entirely within its edict.

The church hierarchy is not surprisingly suspicious of the new system, which lessens the control of the church over schools originally created by the Roman Catholic and Anglican churches themselves for their own members.

In addition to the 15 per cent of intake that the grant-maintained schools are allowed to take as a form of selection in music, modern languages, technology and art, I am surprised that more grant-maintained schools have not brought back further forms of selection. A number of grant-maintained schools recruit on area and siblings with one or two selected classes. Burntwood, a girls' school in Wandsworth with an entry of 280 pupils in 1995, applied last year to have 90 out of the intake chosen on academic grounds each year. Very interestingly, in July 1995 the two Catholic independent schools in the Wirrall both opted to become grant-maintained schools, which was certainly a vote of confidence in the system.

I am, however, not convinced that we have as a Party thought through the grant-maintained schools. I favour them, but if we move to a situation where all schools were grant-maintained it would mean the virtual end of the local education authority and a need to totally rethink how pupils are recruited to schools. If the Conservative Party really believes in spontaneous development and private initiatives it will allow the market to solve itself. Whatever develops would be an improvement on the state direction and planning of the last forty years.

The Prime Minister suggested in 1995 that church schools could become grant-maintained without the need of a parental ballot, that independent schools should be allowed to opt in as grant-maintained schools, and that single-sex grant-maintained schools could change to mixed schools and vice versa. For my part I am totally sympathetic to the Anglican and Catholic hierarchies in opposing any quick fix which would make these schools grant-maintained. Liberty comes from a balance of power and there could be a time when such schools were part of a fight against state direction and in favour of the continuance of a free society. I do not think that the status of these voluntary schools should be changed without an overwhelming vote of parents and the blessing of the church hierarchy.

It is interesting that the Research Director of the Fabians proposed that all schools should be grant-maintained, but this was not supported by the Fabian organization.

Mr Major has also introduced legislation to allow grant-maintained schools, like further education colleges and universities, to borrow against their assets. From April 1997 grant-maintained schools can also keep 100 per cent, as against 50 per cent, of their property disposals.

It is unlikely that within a year of the next general election very many heads and governing bodies will join the queue to become grant-maintained. They will want to know the outcome of the election before committing themselves to such a change. The fact that local financial management has been so successful also lessens the pressure to go grant-maintained.

Mr Blair has chosen to send his son to the Oratory School as against the nearest Catholic school. The Oratory School is now to be allowed to select twenty pupils for their new junior choir by interview and the Labour Party has indicated that it will change its policy on grant-maintained schools by making them foundation schools which will 'hold their own assets, employ their own staff and retain charitable status'. All very interesting.

Mr Major has been radical on education. He said in his Conference Speech, 'So, if parents want specialist schools we should let them have them and if they want religious schools, we should let them have them too.' The weakness of the grant-maintained school system is that the money is paid by the Government to the school directly and not via the consumer, the parent and the pupil's family. If the Government gave each parent a voucher which could be cashed with any school the consumer parent would be in real charge of education in Britain and the free society would have gained another notable victory.

There is a clear gap here between the collectivist and the believer in the free society, which goes back to the first schools being set up for the general public. John Stuart Mill, a classical Liberal, wrote in 1859, 'a general state education is a mere contrivance for moulding people to be exactly like one another'. Two years later the Newcastle Committee reported that parents who were 'destitute of education' were 'just judges of the effective qualities of a teacher'. Contrast these statements with what Professor F. Musgrave wrote in his book *Family, Education and Society* in 1960, 'It is the business of the state in our social democracy to eliminate the influence of parents in the life-chances of the young.'

Twenty-five years ago I thought I had 'discovered' the voucher – the system by which the state gives a voucher to the parent to buy a place in a school. Then I met Ralph (now Lord) Harris of the Institute of Economic Affairs, which had published material in favour of the education voucher. I then read that the Roman Catholic Cardinal Bourne had advocated the voucher in 1926 in Australia and that Tom Paine, author of *The Rights of Man*, had in Virginia, America, in 1790 worked out a method whereby poor families received a grant of £4 for each child under the age of fourteen which they had to spend on education. In 1970 I wrote an introduction to an Institute of Economic Affairs book on the educational voucher, and in 1975 I wrote a pamphlet about it for the Conservative Political Centre and I hoped that it would become official Conservative policy.

When I was an opposition education spokesman for the Conservative Party in 1976 I moved an amendment to Labour's Education Bill of that year as follows: 'On request from a local education authority the Secretary of State shall authorise the establishment of a schools voucher scheme devised and run by the local authority in question, on an experimental basis, for a period of time agreed by the Secretary of State and the authority.' In moving my amendment I said 'that the voucher would fulfil four objectives: it would strengthen the family, it would increase the variety of schools, it would improve general educational standards', and it was 'a means of increasing the choice and control of schools by parents. This is the way in which the education system should go.' I suggested that the voucher should be worth more in downtown areas so that schools competed for deprived children instead of turning them down. I think this was as near as we ever got to having the educational voucher accepted as official Conservative policy. Mr Heath's views, which were sceptical of the educational voucher, were quoted in the debate by the Labour Party, but he and all but one Conservative voted in favour of the amendment, which was lost by 303 to 266 votes.

When we won the 1979 election I took charge of higher education. I was able to influence the party on more parental choice of school and the provision of full information to all parents, but the voucher was a bridge too far. Between 1979 and 1981 the voucher was raised in Parliament by a number of Conservative MPs. On 11 December 1979, in a written reply to a Parliamentary question asking what plans the Government had 'to extend the voucher system in education', I replied: 'My Right Hon. and Learned Friend [Mark Carlisle] has at present no plans to do so. He will watch with interest the progress made by the Kent Education Authority, which intends to mount trial voucher schemes in primary and secondary schools in the next few years.' In similar answers over the next two years there was a clear indication of little Government or Departmental enthusiasm for the voucher.

In 1981 Sir Keith Joseph replaced Mark Carlisle and intellectual debate became the order of the day. I did not believe, however, that anything radical would be done, having seen my loan system for higher education disappear in a few minutes at a Cabinet sub-committee. Sir Keith called an early meeting to discuss the educational voucher. He said he was already tempted to see how open enrolment under the 1980 Act would increase parental choice before going further. I made my views clear that the voucher must not be used for 'topping up' private fees, but must cover the whole cost or it would be killed stone dead as a subsidy to the rich.

Sir Keith indicated his continued interest in the voucher at the 1981 Conservative Party Conference. He then stated on 29 October, in a Parliamentary reply, 'The Government has long been committed to doing everything possible to advance parental choice and parental influence in our school system. . . . However, as I said at the recent Party Conference, I am intellectually attracted to the idea of eventually increasing parental power even further through a voucher system.'

The Department typically drew up a 2,250-word submission on the difficulties of the voucher, which was replied to by Marjorie Selsdon's FEVER (The Friends of the Educational Voucher in Representative Regions), by the National Council for Educational Standards, which I had co-formed years before, by four distinguished scholars, including Professor Milton Friedman, Michael McCrum, the Master of Corpus Christi College, Cambridge, and ex-Headmaster of Eton, Professor Sugarman, Professor Coons and Lord Harris of Highcross. No Departmental reply was given to these submissions. I took advantage, however, of these discussions to support various alternatives, including the right of parents to set up their own schools and then obtain state money, as I had seen in action in Denmark, Holland and other countries. But nothing further happened, and after the general election of 1983 Sir Keith announced at the Conservative Party Conference that the voucher was dead.

It was interesting that at the 1990 Conservative Conference, just before she fell from power, Mrs Thatcher again mentioned the voucher. She commended the pilot scheme for a thousand vouchers for training purposes and said, 'It's the first voucher scheme we've introduced, and I hope it won't be the last.' John MacGregor, then the Secretary of State for Education and Science, commended the vouchers, while Kenneth Clarke condemned them and Mrs Thatcher soon disappeared.

Will the £1,100 nursery vouchers bring vouchers back into fashion?

A second use for educational vouchers could be for sixth-form education, which like nursery education is voluntary. I certainly would still support them, provided we had pilot schemes first to see what the disadvantages were. The voucher as a concept never dies. Indeed it has now appeared in Sweden where Odd Eiken, the Swedish Minister of Schools and Adult Education, had in 1995 given vouchers to parents who wanted their children to attend private schools. The result is that the number of private schools doubled in the last year. Could the Labour Party, in a similar initiative, bring in the educational voucher in Britain as an alternative to the Conservative grant-maintained school should it win the next general election? I doubt it. The Labour Party leaders usually claim more freedom for themselves than they are prepared to give other people.

As things stand it is up to parents and governors whether they become grant-maintained schools or remain under the auspices of the local education authority. I must say that grant-maintained schools that I have visited have been enthusiastic for their new independence and seem to be proud of their new status. The next two years will be critical for the future both of secondary and primary schools in our country and it is to be hoped that a new consensus arises which satisfies the vast majority of our people. Every parent and governor has a part in bringing this about.

The Conservative Party has also given parents a right of appeal if their children are turned down for the school they prefer. Parents have more and more used this right. In 1989–90 there were 20,981 appeals and parents won 43 per cent of them. In 1993–4 the appeals increased to 45,876. This time 41 per cent of appeals were accepted. This led the Labour Party to stress the drop of 2 per cent in accepted appeals, rather than to credit the Government for the fact that more than twice as many parents that year were given on appeal the school that they wished their children to attend.

14

Independent Schools

All free societies are challenged from time to time by movements of an authoritarian nature and it is vital that power and influence must not be concentrated in too few hands, nor must the state have, apart from in defence and possibly law and order, a monopoly. Thus I would defend on 'classical liberal' grounds the right of parents with their own money to decide how their children should be educated, whether these be the 4,000 parents who educate their children at home or those who send their children to small independent schools or those who pay huge fees for the prestigious public schools or the ones in the state sector who are now given the privilege of choosing grant-maintained schools.

In the early 1970s, when so-called permissive and progressive methods were bringing a new dark age into the lives of so many of our children, those of us who were in the state sector fighting for the retention of standards were grateful for the very existence of the independent schools, whose headteachers and parents ensured that true learning did not die.

The better the standard of state education the less likely it is for parents to buy independent education. I remember one public school headmaster saying to me in the early 1960s that public schools would only last one generation because of the improvement – which was then happening at primary and secondary level – in state schools. It was the Labour and Liberal Parties' attack on secondary school selective education and the loony left's attack on all sensible education in the late 1960s which made the public school head's forecast wrong. The disasters in state education at that time were the recruiting sergeants for independent education.

The major public schools provide a first-class attractive education to people not only in Britain but from abroad. English is the world language and the intellectual rigour and the huge choice of extra-curricular activities in the good independent schools are very attractive. In such schools friendships are made which will be of academic, commercial and financial advantage in later years. Academically the prestigious public schools show what good educational standards can achieve. Independent schools took 91 of the first 100 places in the 'A' level league in 1995, and 350 out of the top 600 places. Thirty per cent of independent school applicants to Oxford have at least ABB grades as against 14 per cent from state schools.

It was the destruction of the grammar schools that threw a lifeline to the independent schools. There was a highly effective and informal network between the grammar schools and universities building up in the 1950s and early 1960s which rivalled and in some cases excelled the public school network. A whole generation of professional men, doctors, even university vice-chancellors came to prominence through the grammar schools, whose destruction increased class discrimination in this country. My father, a Labour alderman for forty years, always defended the grammar schools as the ladders of working-class opportunity.

Good discipline and small classes are also the recruiting sergeants for the independent schools. The smaller classes are interesting, since despite evidence abroad that larger, well-disciplined classes are very effective, the public schools still use their small classes as a major attraction for parents.

Independent schools in Britain, with some 600,000 children, have kept their numbers up well during the recession, which has hit and is hitting the middle class heavily. The schools are also affected by the cut in the number of men and women in the armed services, with the loss by parents of boarding allowances. It is likely that over the years the number of boarding independent pupils will fall. Their places are now being partially taken by an increase in overseas boarding students whose parents want them to have a British education.

Recently there have been signs of a new form of independent school, even guaranteeing academic success and giving rebates if examination results are not achieved. Nord Anglia, which originally was an operator of language schools, has now bought a number of private schools and has also won contracts to inspect state schools, run careers services and school advice services. Such organizations could increase further the numbers in independent education by extending the market, and if the intellectual left in Britain destroy the educational chances of children there must always be the freedom to educate children privately here and abroad.

The arrival of the league tables in the national newspapers has not only increased school competition, but has shown families who had previously never thought of private education that money spent on such education would, over a lifetime, be a most rewarding investment. Only a return to further selectivity in the state sector by grant-maintained schools could challenge the independent school dominance of the league tables. As late as 1987 a Mori poll sponsored by *Reader's Digest* was still indicating that 62 per cent of the public would prefer a return to grammar and secondary modern schools and 50 per cent would opt out of the state sector entirely if they could afford it.

15

Higher Education

What is higher education for? Is it for the preservation of high culture or is it for the extended training of minds and skills to allow us to compete economically in an ever more competitive world? If one were a cynic one could also ask if one advantage of increasing the numbers in higher education was not one way of reducing unemployment.

Sir Eric Ashby defined the function of universities as 'preserving, transmitting and enriching culture'. Universities have historically been institutions where scholars met to teach, to discuss, to research and to learn. Their mission has been to seek by all rational means the truth, which can only be found in a setting of free discussion. Matthew Arnold in 1873 defined culture as 'acquainting ourselves with the best that has been known and said in the world, and thus with the history of the human spirit'. Cardinal Newman held that 'The true end of intellectual training and of a University is not in learning or the equivalent but rather in thought or reason exercised upon knowledge'.

At the same time, because of the increase in knowledge and the greater demand for graduates with intellectual skills, students who years ago would never have thought of going to university go there knowing that this is the only real way that they will be accepted for interesting and remunerative employment. Indeed, in some ways the universities have become finishing schools, hopefully with a job ticket at the end of the course.

The numbers in higher education have been greatly increased by the Conservative Government. In 1979 one in eight went on to university; when Mr Major became Prime Minister one in five were going on to higher education and now one in three takes this path. Under Mr Major, through the uprating of polytechnics into universities, we have had the fastest university growth in our history. Between the academic years 1989–90 and 1994–95 numbers in higher education increased by 50 per cent while public support per student declined by 25 per cent. We are now producing more graduates than any other country in Europe except Denmark. Surprisingly enough, when in 1979 I became Minister for Higher Education my remit from Mrs Thatcher was to limit higher education expenditure and to ensure that foreign students who could afford to pay full fees paid them.

In my two years in this post I drew up a partial loans system after visiting the USA, Sweden and other countries to see how their loans systems worked. Mark Carlisle, the Secretary of State for Education and Science, supported the initiative; it was modelled on the Swedish scheme, geared to the tax and social security system, where students paid their loans back over twenty years with incentives for quicker repayment. The scheme disappeared, however, in ten minutes in a Cabinet sub-committee. In politics timing is everything and the timing was wrong! The increase in numbers going on to higher education has brought in a modified loans scheme from 1990 with a pay-back over five years provided that the graduates are earning 85 per cent of the average income. I suspect that unless we discover more North Sea oil, whatever Government is elected at the next general election will over a period of years switch more of the cost of higher education on to loans while decreasing direct grants. The cost of higher education is now around £7.4 billion, a figure too high to be ignored by any Chancellor of the Exchequer. Some 55 per cent of university students take the loans.

I have always supported a system of partial loans and partial grants which encouraged the most able to go on to university, while making the average student think deeply as to whether higher education was the path that he or she should follow. I do believe that the best brains should have every encouragement to go on to further study and research. I would prefer a loans system which could be paid back over twenty years with incentives for earlier repayment. This is basically the Swedish system which is built into the tax system. I would certainly oppose a 'graduate tax' which penalizes the university graduate for the rest of his life and would be a deterrent to many good students. I would also give 100 per cent grants, as well as paying the fees, to the top 5 or 10 per cent of students and let them read whatever subject they wished at university to keep learning and high culture alive while the rest of the students were on a subsidized or full loan system.

After the radical decision of the Conservative Government to give the £1,100 voucher for nursery education, it seems a pity that the Government did not move to a similar radical voucher scheme for higher education. This could have saved money at the same time as it would have given more choice to the student and caused universities to be more radical in their response to student demand. A set voucher, according to the subject, would allow students to decide for themselves whether they wished to live at home cheaply and have minimum debt or whether they wished to live 400 miles away in Halls of Residence at higher expense.

As one who has always enjoyed academic life and study, I have considerable sympathy with the early school leaver who has to pay the living costs and the academic fees for so many students who enjoy the advantages of living away from home. Why should the bus conductor pay towards the tuition fees and part of the keep of the apprentice lawyer who will earn income far beyond that ever to be received by the bus conductor?

Lord Beloff has suggested that our universities are under siege from the philistines of the right and the politically correct of the left. Certainly I shall be surprised if there is not a reassessment of higher education policy after the next general election. Higher education in this country has always gone in cycles of expansion and then critical examination. I suspect the next cycle will be critical examination. I only hope that the correct decisions are then made both for the Exchequer and also for the interests of learning and philosophic enquiry. Certainly the information that in September

1995 at least nine of the ex-polytechnics – now universities – were accepting students at the age of eighteen without any 'A' levels on foundation courses does, as Kingsley Amis once wrote, mean that more will mean worse. I said at the time that pupils who could not pass one or two 'A' levels after two years in the sixth form should go back to school and repeat their last year or take outside employment.

The overall standard of university student recruitment is causing concern. The failure of schools to teach basic mathematics such as multiplication tables is resulting in a university generation unable to cope with science degrees, according to a statement by Dr Tony Gardiner of Birmingham University in September 1995. He said, 'There is a serious problem with mathematics in this country. Without a foundation to build on it is impossible to think on a higher level. We were promised a brave new world of fun attractive mathematics, but the methods were unproven and they have not delivered. Now if you say school children should know about fractions you are accused of being Neanderthal.' At the same time Professor John Hogan of Bristol University said that three recent independent reports had concluded that many schools' teaching of mathematics was very poor.

It is going to be very difficult to keep a level standard of degree between 104 universities, all of whom have different standards of admission and marking of final examinations. The fact also that there is a trend towards modular degrees could make the comparison of degrees between universities very difficult indeed. *The Times* carried a report on 21 September 1995 from the Higher Education Quality Council, which admitted that not all degrees reached the same standard. The more universities there are and the more courses there are within each university the more difficult it will be to standardize degrees, and I suspect that employers will tend to limit their interviews not only to first- and second-class degree holders, but also to Oxford, Cambridge, the London School of Economics, Imperial College and the older civic universities.

Just as we have had slippage in the GCSE examination and the 'A' level examination, the fact that a higher proportion of university students are being awarded first-class honours degrees indicates

89

to the observer that the slippage we have seen at the age of sixteen and eighteen is now occurring at the age of twenty-one. Indeed, over the last ten years there has been a 50 per cent increase in the number of first-class honours degrees being awarded.

There are two more threats to university standards. The first is the risk of the dilution of staff by the newer universities poaching from the older universities by offering professorships. Oxford and Cambridge, because of their living and dining way of life, should not be seriously affected, but the Victorian universities, like Manchester and Birmingham, could easily be affected and one would see the dispersion of top research and lecturing staff all over the country.

The second threat is to the degree system itself. We are now met by rumours that university students will be given school-style reports in place of the traditional degree classifications and that the university vice-chancellors are already considering this since some academics deem our unique system of first-, second- and third-class degrees to be obsolete. At the end of the third year graduates would then be given a detailed report on their skills and knowledge. Yet the present degree system is well understood and this makes it easy for employers to decide who they want to interview and the worthwhileness of a person's degree. There is no way that busy employers want to read detailed reports rather than degree levels, which give an immediate indication as to which graduates they should call for interview.

We used to pride ourselves in Britain that, provided students worked reasonably hard, they had every likelihood of being awarded a good degree. With the almost mass intake to universities the failure rate has increased and one in eight are not now finishing their degrees and are drop-outs, which is not the best way of entering adult life. There is a further problem regarding the universities. There has been a recent decline in the number of students reading language degrees, with a fall of some 42 per cent in German, 26 per cent in French and 21 per cent in Russian. This could be disastrous for our export trade if the decline continues.

The fact that we have two universities now at Oxford must certainly cause difficulties for overseas students, who hope that they are applying and being accepted by the 'real' Oxford University. We have already had Oxford University threatening legal action against a private college recruiting in Canada and offering 'the traditions of Oxford'.

I have always admired John Patten from the days when I first met him when he was a don at Oxford. In spite of this I must state how amazed I was when on one winter's afternoon he announced that all polytechnics would became universities. I wonder what the Conservative Party would have said if it had been in opposition and this comprehensivization of higher education had been put through by the Labour Party. I would follow the suggestion of Lord Beloff that we should have a Premier University League, like the Premier Soccer League. This league should be well funded to ensure British scholarship is kept alive. There is no way that one can keep standards the same with over a hundred universities and fifty other degree-awarding institutions. If our science and scholarship is to be world class we need such a Premier League. How we promote and demote from this League I do not know, but there is always a way where there is a will.

I also think it is time that we had a full review of higher education instead of continued *ad hoc* decisions, which do not put the jigsaw of higher education smoothly together at the present time. The Commission could consider the following issues:

1. The number of students who should be in higher education;
2. The method of funding them by loan and grant;
3. The balance between arts and sciences and commercial subjects;
4. The decline in university salaries, which have dropped by something like 20 per cent relative to other professions in recent years;
5. The fall in engineering students;
6. The fact that for many careers a second degree is now necessary;
7. The 50 per cent increase in first-class degrees as against other degrees.

One could also ask whether the entitlement to a degree course student grant of £1,885 a year and an interest-free loan of £1,385 a year is not too appealing for an eighteen-year-old.

The only trouble with Commissions, as has been said regarding other enquiries, is that they take 'minutes' and last years, by which time the problems are probably totally changed. Nevertheless, I think after the huge increase in university numbers we should assess what is happening and whether it is of advantage both to our country and to learning.

One minor suggestion that could be introduced immediately comes from the university vice-chancellors, who have suggested that admissions tutors should use the applicants' mock 'A' level grades for recruitment without having to wait for the late August results. Apparently mock 'A' levels are much more accurate indicators of the 'A' level grades gained by students than the predictions of the teachers which, to coin a phrase, are 'notoriously inaccurate'!

One must query whether we have got the higher education system right when the demand for science and engineering places is dropping, when De Montfort University spent £400,000 in 1995 on advertising its courses on television and when universities, to keep up their standards, reject poor students and are then financially penalized for their judgement. I also consider that there is something suspect about our higher education system when the University of Salford in 1995 offered £50 in cash to people who recruited a home student and £200 for a non-European Community foreign student. If the drift does continue at first degree level, then able students will have to take a second or even a third degree to establish their academic capabilities.

I fear that following the uprating of the forty-one polytechnics the academic drift that we saw in schools has brought academic drift to what was until recently a tight higher education system. Huddersfield University, having abolished formal examinations, was awarding nearly all its students upper and lower second-class degrees.

The message has, however, got through to students this year that a university degree is not necessarily the key for the future and that the institution that one attends and takes one's degree in is equally important and could be decisive for one's future life. Despite having a larger eighteen-year-old age group applying for university entrance in 1996, there has been a drop in the number of students applying for university. Students are recognizing that degrees from Cambridge, Oxford, Imperial College, University College London, King's College London, Durham and the London School of Economics are very likely to be more respected by future employers than degrees from some of the newly-created universities.

16

The Open University and Adult Education

As a naval volunteer myself in World War II I have always preferred volunteers to pressed men and all my headships were of schools that were always *Oversubscribed*, the title I gave to my book on Highbury Grove. Thus I have always supported voluntary adult education in the name of the Workers' Educational Association and similar bodies. As a schoolboy, with my father and mother, I attended WEA classes and I was a part-time WEA youth lecturer when I left the Royal Navy.

I originally opposed the Open University, believing it to be a Labour Party gimmick. As soon as I was appointed in 1979 as the Minister for Higher Education I visited it. Apart from certain syllabuses, which I thought had left-wing bias, I was impressed by all that I saw and heard. I then visited their summer schools and talked to the students. I was also impressed by the fact that 40 per cent of Open University students were reading sciences, technical subjects and mathematics. I fought very hard in 1981 to keep down the increase of Open University fees. The periodical *Education* reported, 'So this is by way of recording a vote of thanks to a man who clearly believes in pulling one's self up by one's bootlaces.' In 1981 I put forward a scheme to a Cabinet committee to offer part-time students of the Open University interest-free loans, but it was rejected by the Treasury.

I believe that part-time and continuous education are most important for the education and social welfare of the country. Housewives at home, persons with physical disabilities, the fully employed studying in the evening and at weekends must be encouraged to continue their education. They are fully motivated, whereas I suspect that some students carry on in full-time higher education because they fear stepping off the full-time educational ladder.

Adult literacy programmes should also be fully funded. The twenty-year-old who fears the day his fiancée will discover he is semi-illiterate or the father who is illiterate and whose child will soon ask him for help with his reading is as much deserving of government help as anybody in the land. Indeed, since they were the failures of an educational system which never gripped them they deserve all our help.

I now know very many people, some of conservative opinions and even Conservative Party members, who have taken Open University degrees, and on financial cost grounds they saved the country large amounts of money by studying part-time as against going up automatically to full-time university degree courses. One subject on which I agree with the late Harold Wilson is that of the Open University. All parents and governors who have sufficient time should enquire from the Open University about courses or degrees that will help them in their work and in their general life.

I still have a soft spot for the WEA classes. With its 700 branches, 10,000 courses and some 156,000 students, the Association still provides a very necessary liberal feel to our further education system, with its emphasis on 'learning for pleasure'. Eighty-five per cent of WEA students follow liberal studies and there is no doubt my parents will be sitting on the front row when I join my first WEA class in the next world.

17

Education, Identity and Political Correctness

Children must grow up with a sense of identity, aware of who they are and the history of their village, town, county, country and the world outside. We start with the 'little platoons' of Edmund Burke and end with the United Nations and how we can preserve our world and our environment.

We must start with our own roots and achievements as a people. We have a great deal to be proud of: the growth of democracy over so many centuries, the rule of law, our sea history, the Industrial Revolution which first happened in Britain, our literature and the arts, World War I and World War II and the voluntary end of Empire and our continued friendship with the ex-colonial powers, especially India. This history should be taught in the round, warts and all!

We also need heroes to show young people what they can achieve. If we do not proffer such heroes then people will create their own. Nature abhors a vacuum, and soccer and pop stars will become the examples for our young people.

Nicholas Tate, the Chief Executive of the Schools Council and Curriculum Assessment Authority, has stated that without a unified culture our society will break up. The immigration to Britain since the end of World War II is of people who wished to come to this country and, whilst preserving their various cultures, wished to be British. They came here because they like our freedoms and the rule of law and because we came together at the time of Empire. Indeed Britain and India have never been as close as they are now. I am proud to be British and to have served in His Majesty's Forces in World War II and afterwards, and I trust that the citizens of other countries are similarly proud of their countries.

I am a fundamentalist as against a behaviourist. I believe there are certain values that must be taught in schools: truth, respect for others, fair dealing, service before self. A good family, a good school, a good regiment, a good church will teach such values to its members. Plato and Aristotle considered that the aims of education should be ethical, and Cardinal Newman believed we should teach 'a philosophic habit of mind'. Life is not all relative. There are absolutes which should be taught and which we must strive to fulfil. There are also real heroes in life such as the Pope, Nelson Mandela, the Queen. Young people need models or they will take up others which are not as good.

I realize that in eleven years of compulsory schooling we cannot teach the whole of British and world history, but history teaching must be coherent. I do not think that short modular six-week courses on, say, the Roman army, the Norman Conquest, medieval England, the English Civil War, the Boer War is as helpful as teaching over the eleven years from simple pre-history up to and beyond World War II. I was certainly shocked that half of our children did not know who Winston Churchill was when questioned at the time of the fiftieth anniversary of the end of World War II. Without his leadership there would have been no Britain for such young people to live in and they should know this.

Lord Blake holds that our history is our natural identity, yet history is no longer compulsory to the age of sixteen. Instead we now have in certain schools political correctness, which often means the rewriting of history according to the fashions of our time.

One local education authority has introduced the teaching of sexual equality to three-year-olds. This is the death of the age of innocence and childhood despite the good intentions of the creators of such courses. I would repeat that the world goes out in collective circles from the family, which itself is now under threat, to the village or community neighbourhood unit, the town, the county, the country and the world.

The schoolmaster or schoolmistress and the teacher cannot solve all the problems of mankind, but I was proud to have been for twenty-three years a schoolteacher and a headmaster and a member of such a great profession. To teach children is a privilege and an honour and one of the most enjoyable of occupations in the world. I enjoy giving my job description these days as Member of Parliament and schoolmaster. My father would prefer the first but my mother undoubtedly would prefer the second.

18

Political Parties

Until recently the Labour Party's education policies were a major vote loser. They failed to take up Prime Minister Callaghan's challenge in his Ruskin College speech of 18 October 1976, where he admitted that the policies of his Party were not delivering what parents wanted, especially in the basic skills of literacy and numeracy. Most of the Labour Party's spokesmen and women continued up to late 1994 to advocate policies that were anathema to the majority of our people. I had thought in 1976 that the Labour Party would take up the torch of the need for a return to a national curriculum while the Conservatives would become the party of parental choice. Amazingly the Labour Party allowed the Conservatives to take and keep both torches. Parents want choice of school, but they also want a basic national curriculum so that their children can be geographically and socially mobile.

Thus from 1979 onwards the Conservatives took Act after Act through the British Parliament extending parental choice of school, the right of parents to know the curriculum and examination results of local schools, and an appeal system when pupils did not get the school of their choice. Schools were put under the control of parents and teacher governors and could, after the 1988 Act, even opt out of local control to become grant-maintained schools. All these changes were popular with parents, yet the Labour Party fought them line by line because the Labour Party still represented the producers and not the consumers of the educational process.

It has taken the arrival of Mr Blair as the Leader of the Labour

99

Party to partially change this. As a parent he chose for his son to go to the London Oratory, a distinguished grant-maintained school. He has since, on 23 June 1995, attacked the progressive teaching methods that for a generation have failed our children and their parents. He called for more vigorous teaching of the three Rs, a return to grouping by ability, more formal whole-class teaching and the 'modernizing' of the comprehensive system.

Mr Blair added, 'For some on the Left, to talk of pressure on schools, teachers and pupils is to sell the pass. . . . For me this typifies the reasons why the Left has been losing general elections for the last sixteen years instead of winning them. . . . The people who suffer from lack of pressure are not the well-off and the articulate. Instead the losers are precisely the people who most need a hand-up in life because they were not born with natural advantages. . . . It is traditional Labour voters who lose out when teaching is poor, discipline non-existent, and the culture one which excuses low standards on grounds of background or disadvantage. . . . What these parents want is the best possible education for their children. They are right to demand more than we currently deliver.'

In a speech later that day he also said, 'Mixed-ability teaching is not an end in itself. Children who are good at maths can benefit from being taught with other children good at maths. And for some classes they should be. . . . On the Left, low performance was often blamed on socio-economic factors. It neglected the fact that schools clearly make a difference to a child's education, and different schools with similar intakes can produce markedly different results.'

So where do we go from there? Certainly this could allow a new dialogue in British educational politics and we can talk about the future instead of being obsessed with the past. There has also been the mention of specialist schools such as music, science, design and mathematics schools as against the blanket comprehensive system so beloved of old Labour.

Sadly, the Labour Party publication *Diversity and Excellence: A New Partnership for Schools,* issued in autumn 1995, has many of the signs of unreconstructed Old Labour. It is a cleverly written document to try to keep the Labour Party in line. Attacks on the grant-maintained schools are out, but they are going to be weakened in their independence by two local authority nominees sitting on each governing body, their admissions procedure has to be agreed with the local education authority, and no longer can they approach the Education and Employment Department to change their entry policies.

The other schools will be aided schools, which are the present church schools, and community schools, which are the present county schools. The Funding Agency for Schools which now funds grant-maintained schools will be abolished and the funding will be devolved to local education authorities under whatever funding criteria are eventually agreed. I do not believe that the grant-maintained schools will have a thanksgiving party for that sentence. A commitment is made that instead of the minimum 85 per cent of local authority money being devolved to schools, in future 90 per cent will be devolved, which will please the ex-county schools but not the grant-maintained schools, which already receive a 100 per cent grant.

In parts of the document *Diversity and Excellence* we see the old Labour Party obsessed by the one issue it could agree on – opposition to the 11-plus examination. We read: 'we are implacably opposed to a return to selection at 11-plus', 'We oppose any return to selection through the 11-plus', 'Our opposition to academic selection at 11 has always been clear.'

I accept that no party would bring back the old 11-plus, but it is as well to remember that this examination brought more working-class children to universities in Britain than the percentage of working-class children attending universities anywhere else in Europe. The 11-plus examination was replaced in very many areas by an 11-plus selection by the neighbourhood in which one lived, where the suburban school was really a grammar school with a short tail of less able pupils, while the downtown secondary modern school in the inner city had few, if any, ladders of opportunity.

I like the sentence in the Labour document, 'Parental preference is denied where selection by examination is employed.' So what – a national lottery every Saturday night with the prize of pupils being helicoptered out of the inner-city forlorn-hope school?

We were also informed by Mr Blunkett at the 1995 Labour Party

Conference, which voted to abolish grant-maintained schools, that foundation schools would not be allowed to interview parents and children, apart from interviewing parents regarding the religious convictions of their children. The privilege given to Mr Blair and tens of thousands of other parents by actually cross-examining the headteacher about the aims and curriculum of the school will end and another part of the secret garden of education which has been opened up by the Conservative Party will become secret again. Such restrictions on interviewing pupils and parents, the local authority control of admissions policy and the cut of 10 per cent in their funding will certainly mean teacher redundancies and the end of the successful grant-maintained schools.

If there are to be no interviews of parents and pupils we shall either have neighbourhood schools or bussing. The former will be in many cases one-class schools, the latter will be as unpopular in Britain as it was in America, and in neither case will there be any real parental choice. The downtown school will be virtually a secondary modern with a GCSE stream, and the up-market school will be a grammar school with a bottom stream of low achievers. *The Times* leader of 5 October 1995 commented, 'Relative Victory. Blair's education policy is better for Labour than for Britain.' We shall be interested to see how Mr Blair's educational policies develop if he is allowed to continue them. The history of the Labour Party over the last twenty-five years throws doubt on this, since the comprehensive school has often been the only policy with which all people in the Labour Party can agree.

Later in 1995 the Labour Party published another document, *Excellence for All*, which, along with speeches from Mr Blair and Mr Blunkett and his team, took the Labour Party towards the middle ground of educational politics. The 11-plus seems to be forgotten and there is hardly a mention of a defence of the comprehensive school. Instead it is accepted that Britain has fallen behind countries like France, Germany and Japan. Even the decline in apprenticeships is sadly mentioned.

A General Teaching Council is commended to raise the standard of teaching and there is to be a 'new grade of Advanced Skills

Teacher', whereby the best teachers can be rewarded within the classroom. There are also to be teacher sabbaticals.

Ineffective heads and teachers are to be replaced and the maximum number in a primary school class must be no more than thirty. Tests are allowed for five-year-olds, 'setting' is mentioned and there is to be homework for all pupils rising from half an hour for the seven- to eleven-year-olds to one and a half hours for the secondary school pupils. Sin bins are to be allowed, contracts with teachers recommended and a new qualification brought in for teachers to sit before they can apply for headships.

There is also the suggestion that primary school pupils should learn a foreign language, which is one of the few 'trendy' suggestions in *Excellence for All*. Every ten or twenty years such foreign language innovation is suggested, brought in and then dispensed with again. I think the Labour Party would be better advised to concentrate on primary school literacy and numeracy.

Occasionally the old Labour Party comes in. We read in *Excellence for All*, 'The gap in educational achievements mirrors the growing divide between rich and poor.' The real gap in educational achievements, however, is between trendy teachers who have betrayed their pupils in downtown city schools and traditional teachers who have tried in all areas to prepare their pupils for maximum achievements. The whole question of selection by ability and interest within the existing comprehensive schools is ignored. Here the Labour Party faces the past and not the future.

Mr Blunkett said at the 1995 Labour Party Conference, 'Let me say this very slowly indeed. Watch my lips: no selection by examination or interview under a Labour Government.' So there the Labour Party remains trapped in its old socialist identity, condoning selection not by ability but by the home you come from, the area in which you can afford to buy a house and the income of your parents. The caterpillar trying to become a butterfly finds its wings cut before it can even fly.

Following the episode when Harriet Harman chose for her child a grant-maintained grammar school well away from her home, the Labour Party indicated that the destruction of the remaining grammar schools would only occur if the feed primary school parents of such schools so wished it. Alas, there was no commitment that the parents of children in the area of a comprehensive school would be allowed to vote for secondary selective schools in their area. The Labour Party still has a one-way system which would destroy selective grant-maintained schools of which most parents approve and of which many Labour Party members take advantage.

It is important that governors and parents make their decisions regarding school policy and regarding their own children according to their own views and not those of the political parties to which they belong. Highbury Grove was a classic example of a school where the parents put the educational opportunities of their children before their political views, but that courage is not often seen in this country. I do believe, however, that more and more parents and governors are concerned about the issues and not who puts the policy forward, and this is a welcome advance.

The educational policies of the Liberal Democrats, however, fully outpoint the policies of the Labour Party in other-worldliness and banality. Headed, like the Labour Party's policy, *Excellence for All*, the paper promises 'fully democratically elected Local Education Departments', extra funding for schools and a 'participation for pupils, students and staff in the running of education establishments through automatic voting representation on governing bodies to democratic school councils, student unions and staff organisations'. This sounds like the worst excesses of the Red Guards in China and the way the Inner London Education Authority towards its end tried to run its schools.

The Liberal Democrats would abolish the assisted places scheme and the grant-maintained schools and its policy hints at the end of the remaining grammar schools. As for entry into comprehensive schools, it would 'Lay down clear criteria on every comprehensive school, while opposing any move towards selection on the grounds of ability or class'. One of the few clear commitments would be to 'provide nursery education for every three or four year old whose parents want it'. Oh yes, there is also the mention of opposition to bullying – that will put every parent's mind at rest!

19

Educational Comparisons with Other Countries

The first comparison of educational standards was possibly by Xenophon in the fourth century BC, when in *Cyropaedia* he compared Persian with Spartan education. It was then and is still now a very inexact science.

The 1990 second International Assessment of Educational Progress (IAEP) at the ages of nine and thirteen, which covered twenty countries, put Korea, Taiwan, Hungary and Switzerland as the leading school achievers and linked this with the amount of homework set in these countries and the smaller amount of television watched. Another survey of numeracy in 1978–82 and in 1987 showed that English children were below average in arithmetic but ahead in geometry, and the gap between the best and the worst scholars in Britain was wider than that in other countries. The British 1970 birth cohort, when checked in 1991, showed that 15 per cent had limited literacy skills, 3 per cent did not wish to read but only 1 per cent were actually illiterate. The Taiwanese children have frequent tests, homework every day and they attend extra classes in the evening and at weekends.

The international school effectiveness project, which tested 2500 children from eight countries, put Taiwan and Hong Kong in the top slots, both in arithmetic and the use of mathematics. The other countries were Holland, Australia, Canada and Norway. England was fourth in arithmetic and sixth in the use of mathematics.

Interestingly enough, classes of forty-plus performed excellently if taught as a whole and where the teacher was effective. Despite the continued decrease over many years in the size of class and the fact that British children now stay two years longer in school than in 1945, there seems little change in the literacy and numeracy scores of our schoolchildren. Size of class certainly does not seem to matter.

Prais and Wagner (1983) compared mathematics test results of West German and English secondary schools and found that 'the level of attainment of the lower half of German pupils was higher than the average level of attainment in England'. Postlethwaite's 1988 study concluded that 'in the sciences English 14 years olds scored lower than their peers in all 17 countries compared'. Lynn (1988) reviewed the scores of thirteen-year-olds on international mathematics achievement tests and found that 'approximately 79 per cent of Japanese children obtained a higher score than the average English child'.

David Finegold and David Soskice reported that 'the combination of poor performance during the compulsory years and a high percentage of students leaving school at 16 has meant that the average English worker enters employment with a relatively low level of qualifications' when compared to Germany, France, Japan and the USA.

The recent publication *Productivity, Education and Training* by Professor Sig Prais shows that thirteen-year-olds in England are outscored by those in France, Italy and Switzerland and that the underscoring in mathematics was very serious indeed. England could only claim to be marginally ahead of the USA, while it was far behind other countries.

Last year the London Mathematical Society called for a Government enquiry into the 'disastrous state' of teaching in the subject. Figures were quoted in October 1995 which showed that the mathematical ability of English thirteen-year-olds had fallen well below that of children of the same age from Finland, Greece, Holland and Singapore. David Burghes, Professor of Mathematical Education at Exeter University, said that 'England had gone too far down the road of child-centred learning at the expense of chanting tables and studying in a disciplined way'. He added, 'Teachers are not to blame, but we need to get back to whole-class lessons and limit the use of calculators, which is encouraged from primary school upwards.' David Burghes added that he found the Singaporean thirteen-year-olds were twice as likely to get the right answer to a numerical question as English children.

Britain is almost alone in Europe and the Far East in having what is virtually a total comprehensive secondary school system in the State sector. Germany sends one-third of its children to the equivalent of grammar schools, about a half to technical schools (Realschulen) and the rest to general secondary schools which are of a very high standard. In Germany there is also specialization within the selective system. There are often separate schools which specialize in classics, modern languages, mathematics and natural science where the best teachers in these subjects and the best pupils are brought together.

Russia has some of the most highly selective schools in the world. I was once visited by a headmaster from Moscow who selected some fifty pupils a year for their mathematical ability from a population of five million. They were taught largely by mathematics graduates from Moscow University, which has a very high mathematical reputation. Russia did not get into outer space by a nonselective secondary school system, but by giving every opportunity at an early age to their most able pupils. Russia has some 30–35 per cent in technical and trade schools.

Switzerland has four types of school: the Oberschulen with 5–10 per cent of the children of the lowest ability, the Realschulen for the next 30–35 per cent, some 40–45 per cent go to the Sekundarschulen, with 10–15 per cent being selected to the equivalent of the German Gymnasium. Swiss schools are small and intimate with usually only 300 pupils in a secondary school (less in primary schools). The form teacher, apart from in the Gymnasium, teaches a wide range of subjects to his class for three or more years. Specialist teaching only occurs in the Gymnasium, yet the average pupil reaches the equivalent of grammar school standards in Britain and we have three times as many low achievers. In Switzerland there is little 'work at your own pace', which generally means 'doing as little as you can get away with'. Similarly in science it is generally the teacher who does the experiment and the class who watches. I can well remember the hours that I semi-wasted (as a pupil!) in so-called experiments in the chemistry laboratory of Haslingden Grammar School. We worked in twos at the laboratory benches and when I read up in the evening what was supposed to have been done in the daytime, it was clear that my own experiments had rarely been a great success but had absorbed very much time!

Japan has probably the most tested children in the world. They are systematically taught to read and write from the age of six and have extra holiday work if they fall behind. Again it is whole-class teaching. Ninety-two per cent of children in Japan stay until at least the age of eighteen. The Japanese school day is longer than in Britain and supplementary teaching is given at weekends and in the holidays. Japanese teachers all teach to the average of the class with no concessions for mixed abilities. Japanese pupils also clean the school for twenty minutes before going home in the afternoon. The French school day is also longer. Sixth-form pupils in Britain are taught for eighteen hours a week, which compares with thirty hours of tuition for arts students in France and thirty-six hours for French science students.

Whatever one's views on school arrangements and organization, there is little doubt that whole-class teaching aimed at just above the average is the most effective teaching method. It also helps to set and mark regular homework and to limit the number of hours of television watching allowed to children.

Such societies, as in Taiwan, Japan, Korea and Hungary, all of which I have visited, have 'a learning culture' which is certainly not endemic in Britain at the present time.

There seems little relationship between the amount of the gross national product spent on education and educational achievement. Canada spends 6.7 per cent of its GNP on education, Sweden 6.5 per cent, the United Kingdom 5.3 per cent, Germany 4 per cent and Japan 3.7 per cent. Nor, having seen the large classes in the Far East, do smaller classes seem to be of any advantage. Indeed the opposite seems to be the case. Where a teacher has a large class he or she will insist on discipline and all the class working together, whereas when there is a small class this is sub-divided even more into group teaching or even individual teaching with a lower standard of discipline and the class teacher becomes a social friend rather than an objective teacher. It is the same in the United Kingdom. Often the lowest pupil/teacher ratios have the worst results. Lambeth and Waltham Forest, whom the Inspectors concluded have let down their children, are very heavy spenders.

The Conservative Government has a good record in educational expenditure if this is considered an educational advantage. Baroness Miller, speaking in November 1995 in the House of Lords, gave a series of interesting figures. Spending on teachers had risen by some 50 per cent in real terms since 1979; there were 135 per cent more support staff in our schools; expenditure on books and equipment had gone up by 55 per cent. Fewer than 30 per cent of primary school pupils were in classes of over 30 as compared with 35 per cent in 1979.

Britain has to face up to the truth regarding its educational record. At the North of England Conference in January 1996, Sir Geoffrey Holland, a former Permanent Secretary at the Department of Education and Employment, told the Conference that our education ranked only 35th in the world in its effectiveness. That is a worrying figure.

20

How Do We Improve Educational Standards?

What must we do to improve British educational standards? The first answer is to see the position exactly as it is: to realize how far we have fallen behind other countries in educational standards where we can compare them. There must be no fudging of this.

Any disparity has nothing to do with the pupil-teacher ratio or the size of class, despite the fact that 89 per cent of the public favour smaller classes and despite the fact that one of the selling points for private and public schools in Britain is that their class sizes are smaller than in the State sector. I have seen mixed-ability classes being taught mathematics in South Korea, Japan and Taiwan, and these classes had an average size of 49, 45 and 40 respectively.

Interestingly enough, according to the statistics of January 1995, the grant-maintained schools in outer London had an average pupil-teacher ratio of 26.3 pupils per class while the local authority schools in outer London had a pupil-teacher ratio of only 17.1 pupils per teacher, yet there is no shortage of pupils wishing to join grant-maintained schools in the London area, and parents have plenty of confidence in the standard of these schools.

Since teachers are paid a set salary irrespective of the size of class taught, they will obviously always continue to advocate smaller classes since this makes their task much easier. It would be interesting to change the teachers' salary arrangements so that teachers were paid according to the number of pupils they taught in a week or a month. I would not be in the least surprised if teachers then found that they could teach much bigger classes than the ones they have now.

When I was Headmaster of Highbury Grove School under the Inner London Education Authority I always considered that I could have run an even better school if I could have dispensed with the least able quarter of my teachers and increased the salaries of the other teachers by a third.

As far back as the Black Paper days I considered that smaller classes were used to introduce ineffective group teaching as against teaching of the whole class, which is the norm in the Far East and in the rest of Europe. If a class is taught in four groups in a forty-minute lesson only ten minutes' teaching is given to each pupil. This is a waste of pupil and teacher time.

The vast number of classes in Britain are of a size below 30 pupils. In January 1995 70 per cent of primary school classes and 93 per cent of secondary school classes were below 30. The comparative figures in 1979 were 65 per cent and 84 per cent. Class sizes are increasing at the present time, but if this forces teachers to teach the whole class together this could be an advantage rather than a disadvantage.

Homework is also very important. Each school should have its own homework policy decided by teachers and parents. All pupils should have homework books which are signed daily by parents and by teachers. The time spent on such homework should always be listed. Parents should ensure that the television watching of their children is not excessive. Many young people now spend twenty-five hours a week watching television. Normal television is certainly not an educative factor, but more a drug, and any learning is generally disconnected and accidental.

In Britain a fifth of school leavers leave at sixteen, seventeen and eighteen with no qualifications at all and with an educational achievement below that of an average eleven-year-old pupil. There is a great need for a new examination at fifteen or sixteen that guarantees basic literacy and numeracy, the ability to concentrate and to have a basic body of knowledge. The peak of truancy is from the age of fourteen to sixteen. If pupils spend two years truanting from fourteen to sixteen they are likely to be unemployable for life because the habits of punctuality and hard work will be totally dissipated. OFSTED considers that between 500 and 2500 schools are failing their pupils at the present time.

I must add, however, that I have a degree of cynicism about any inspection system where the inspector is advised to inform the head teacher as to which staff are failing. If a headmaster or a headmistress cannot themselves identify which staff in their schools are failing without the advice of an inspector the sooner that head returns to classroom teaching the better!

Do we spend too much time in school on foreign languages, particularly bearing in mind that the international language is now English and is likely to remain so for our lifetime? Certainly too many children learn French just because there are plenty of French teachers. More children should learn Chinese, Japanese, Russian, Spanish. . . . Unless children and young people really learn languages to a proficient level, such lessons are probably a waste of time.

The discovery method of teaching has done untold harm to British education. Schools are for teaching and if pupils could learn for themselves there would be no point in having expensive schools. 'Teachers should be teachers and not facilitators,' as John Clare once wrote. Cross-curriculum teaching has been another fashion that brought deterioration in its wake.

The retreat from phonic teaching has lowered the reading standards of our country and the sooner all infant school children are taught from the start by the phonic method the better. By all means use 'look and say' and 'real books' occasionally and for specific children, but the phonic method is the one that has been historically most effective. Although it is probably the most time-consuming for teachers, it is the most time-achieving for pupils. Most of the so-called modern methods have been invented for bored teachers and not bored pupils!

I have referred elsewhere to the efficiency of the emergency training scheme for teachers after World War II, where student teachers were taught by heads and deputy heads on secondment who actually knew what the classroom was like and how to succeed in it. I have found in the Far East the same mature attitude among many teachers. For instance, if the teacher is by the blackboard and stands on a platform four to six inches high he or she can dominate the room.

I also think that the dispersal of teacher trainees in different university and college faculties is a mistake. Trainee teachers should, wherever possible, be taught together, like medical students, since this makes all the difference in group morale and pride.

League tables have shown that even in the worst areas there are heads and teachers who enthuse their pupils while in the best catchment areas there will be failing schools. The key to a good school is a purposeful head. Schools are like ships; no good if the captain keeps looking back. The headteacher is also like the soccer manager – he must lead and give inspiration to his team.

The pattern in the State sector of deputy heads becoming heads is an unfortunate one. A deputy headteacher has to ensure that all goes smoothly in the school and all ends are tied up. The headteacher is the one who gives the direction. Many good deputy headteachers who can ensure the routine efficient running of a school have not the flair for the captain's post and their schools are very humdrum. I suspect that public schools choose their headteachers because of their drive and vision and not because they were good deputy heads elsewhere. My achievements at Highbury Grove came largely because I had two deputy heads with long experience to whom I could leave the daily running of the school while I could give drive and vision to the whole staff. Sadly both of these men are now dead, yet, after twenty years, I still miss my talks with them and the great loyalty they gave to me and the pitfalls of over-enthusiasm from which they saved me.

The USA is another country where the educational achievements have not equalled the money spent. In the last ten years expenditure on education in America has increased by 126 per cent with little improvement of standards. The money has been wasted on a soft curriculum, radical ideology, psychological rubbish and even the shortening of school hours. Spending per pupil in American schools is now $6404 per pupil, which far exceeds the $4100 being spent by many families buying private education in many states in America.

One final but important issue is selection. The Labour Party is still ambiguous regarding selection of pupils according to their different abilities. Throughout Europe and the Far East there is a distinctive belief in selective education. Children are different emotionally and intellectually. At some stage there has to be some form of selection for the sake of the very able, the average and the less able. This is not a moral issue but a pragmatic one if children are to reach their highest potential. To educate very able children in their teens along with less able children will make the able arrogant and the least able despondent. Such educational organization is also highly inefficient. At some stage and in some way there has to be fair and open selection. If we do not face this in our country then we will continue to damage our children and our society, and some day both the Labour Party and the Conservative Party will have to face up to this if educational standards in Britain are to be improved.

The improvement of British education depends basically upon two words – 'will' and 'discipline'. The headmaster must be in charge of the school and the teacher must be in charge of the classroom. If they are not they should be sacked.

Classes should be taught as a whole with a distinct and known syllabus in every subject. The pupils should also sit at desks or tables in an order decided by the teacher. All school work should be marked and homework set every evening. Classes should generally work in silence, apart from the teacher. There should be frequent tests and extra work for any who fall behind.

Tidiness, courtesy and punctuality should be the order of every day and parents sent for in cases of misdemeanour or falling behind in work. Poor home standards should never be accepted as an excuse for poor school standards either in work or behaviour.

The Conservative Government has over seventeen years done a great deal to open up the secret garden of education, but we still need even greater openness of information and decision and we certainly must accept that we have made great mistakes in education over the last forty years. Defensive thinking by teacher unions or by political parties will certainly do us no good.

As I write this last paragraph I am reminded that the local education authority with the largest class sizes in November 1995 topped the National League Tables for GCSE results, becoming the first local education authority to record a pass rate of more than 55 per cent of pupils gaining A to C grades. Ironically, the Liberal Democrats are now in control of the Kingston-upon-Thames Guildhall and are committed to reducing the size of class! Presumably this will be to ensure that they do not top the League in educational achievement again.

APPENDIX
INFORMATION FOR GOVERNORS
AND PARENTS

How to Choose a School for Your Child

(1) Read the prospectuses of local schools.

(2) Visit local schools by appointment.

(3) If your child is already in school talk with other parents as to their views of local schools.

(4) Similarly, if your child is already in school talk to his/her present headteacher and also the present class teacher regarding local schools.

(5) Talk with your neighbours, people at your place of worship and other societies about their views of local schools.

(6) Check if local schools have open days for potential parents.

(7) Obtain the school performance tables, which are published each November. Each local education authority has a booklet which helps you to compare the local schools.

(8) Certainly at secondary school level check the curriculum of the schools and see what specialities there are in science and languages.

(9) Check the National Curriculum Assessment results, subject by subject.

(10) Check the public examination results, subject by subject in the secondary schools.

(11) Check which sports are played and what other hobbies are catered for inside the school.

(12) Check how many parents applied for their children to go to the schools in previous years and how many were accepted.

(13) Stand at the school gate, disguised as a tree, and watch how fast pupils enter in the morning and how slowly they come out at the end of the day. If at 4 p.m. the pupils are knocked over by staff rushing away from the school, disappear for your own safety and thank your lucky stars that your child is not in such a school.

(14) The sophisticated test – if taken round the school check the angle of the head of the pupils in the classes: if they are at 60° they are learning, if they are at 30° they are sleeping and if they are at 100° they are in revolt – known as Boyson's Law.

If your child is refused a place in the school of your choice ask immediately how many are on the waiting list in front of your son or daughter before you decide your next move.

If your child has been put in for a local authority or grant-maintained school you can appeal against an adverse decision, and in 41 per cent of the cases parents have won.

Basic Information for Parents and Governors

Nursery School	3–5 years
Infant School	5–7 years
Junior School	7–11 years
Middle School	8–12 or 13 years
Secondary School	11–18 years
Local Authority School	Controlled by local authority.
Voluntary Controlled School	Under church control but funded overwhelmingly by the local education authority.
Voluntary Aided School	Under firm church control but with less local authority input than voluntary controlled schools.
Grant-maintained School	Funded directly by Government.
Secondary Grammar School	Selective school controlled by the local authority – can be grant-maintained.

City Technology College	Self-standing school set up by the Government, funded directly by Government with the support of local industry.
OFSTED	The Office for Standards in Education, which will arrange four-yearly inspections of all schools.
Vouchers	A means of financing education by giving parents vouchers of a specific value with which they buy places in schools for their children. This puts the parents in charge of schools.
Nursery Vouchers	These have been introduced in four education authorities for nurseries only, whereby parents buy half full-time nursery education. They are valued at £1,100 each.

Constitution of Governing Bodies for LEA Schools

	Up to 99 pupils	100–299 pupils	300–599 pupils	600+ pupils
Elected parents	2	3	4	5
LEA appointees	2	3	4	5
Elected teachers	1	1	2	2
Co-optees (foundation)	3 (2)	4 (3)	5 (4)	6 (4)
Head (if he/she chooses)	1	1	1	1

Co-options of Governors in local authorities will be chosen from all sections of the local community including businessmen.

In voluntary controlled schools the majority of those co-opted will come from the school's foundation members, usually from the local church.

In voluntary aided schools the governing body is made up of a majority of foundation governors, but still has representatives from the local education authority, parents and teachers and, where there is a Parish Council, one representative from the Parish Council.

People are allowed to serve on only two governing bodies.

A governor can be disqualified if he does not attend governors' meetings for six months.

How to Become a Grant-maintained School

(1) The governors of the school pass a resolution or 20 per cent of the parents sign if they wish to change to a grant-maintained school.

(2) Within ten weeks a ballot is then held, which is a secret ballot with voting by post; if then less than 50 per cent vote there has to be a second ballot. If the ballot is affirmative for grant-maintained status it goes for approval to the Secretary of State for Education.

(3) Grant-maintained schools can only change their admissions procedure with the consent of the Secretary of State for Education and Employment – he or she can give permission for selective intakes of various types.

(4) Grant-maintained schools must do the national curriculum, which is voluntary in the private sector. They can, however, ask the Secretary of State to given them dispensation from parts of the national curriculum or even send an alternative curriculum for Government approval.

Appendix

National Tests in Schools

SEVEN-YEAR-OLDS

There are writing, reading, spelling and arithmetic tests covering three hours.

ELEVEN-YEAR-OLDS

They have tests in English, mathematics and science covering four and a half hours.

FOURTEEN-YEAR-OLDS

Again they are tested in English, mathematics and science, and the tests at this age last approximately six and three-quarter hours.

There are various levels of tests, from Level 2 for typical seven-year-olds to Level 5 and 6 for fourteen-year-olds. The core curriculum is now English, mathematics and science in all schools, with the addition of Welsh in Wales. The foundation subjects are now technology, geography, history, a modern language (in secondary schools only), art, music, physical education and religious education along with the daily assembly, which is still mandatory.

Appendix

External Examinations

'O' level grades	CSE grades	GCSE grades
—	—	A*
A	—	A
B	—	B
C	1	C
D	2	D
E	3	E
U	4	F
—	5	G

GCSEs are awarded in grades A* (highest) to G. The General Certificate of Secondary Education (GCSE) is now taken by most children.

There is also the Advanced Level General Certificate of Education ('A' level), which is graded A–E, as above, with additional grades N (narrow failure) and U (unclassified).

The Advanced Supplementary Level of the GCE in each subject is worth half an 'A' level.

There is a degree level which covers fifteen areas in business, social work and leisure activities, and there are National Vocational Qualifications (NVQs) which are parallel with the 'A' level courses.

Further Reading

List of abbreviations and addresses

CPS: Centre for Policy Studies (52 Rochester Row, London SW1P 1JU)

CRE: Campaign for Real Education (18 Westlands Grove, Stockton Lane, York Y03 OEF)

ERC: Educational Research Centre (Sherwood Press, 88 Tylney Road, London E7)

IEA: Institute of Economic Affairs (2 Lord North Street, London SW1P 3LB)

IEA Education Unit: Warlingham Park School, Chelsham Common, Warlingham, Surrey CR3 9PB

IEDDS: Institute of European Defence and Strategic Studies (13–14 Golden Square, London W1)

Research Publications: PO Box 39850, Phoenix, Arizona 85969, USA

SAU: Social Affairs Unit (Suite 5/6, Morley House, 314–322 Regent Street, London W1R 5A)

Further Reading

Anderson, Digby (ed.), *Education for Employment?* (SAU, 1982)

——, *Full Circle? Bringing Up Children in the Post-Permissive Society* (SAU, 1988)

——, *Trespassing? Businessmen's Views on the Educational System* (SAU, 1984)

——, *Detecting Bad Schools: A Guide for Normal Parents* (SAU, 1982)

Beattie, Alan, *History in Peril: May Parents Preserve It* (CPS, 1987)

Bierhoff, Helvia, and S. J. Prais, *Schooling as Preparation for Life and Work in Switzerland and Britain* (NIESR, 1995)

Blumenfeld, Samuel L., *NEA: Trojan Horse in American Education* (Research Publications, 1990)

Boyson, Rhodes, *Crisis in Education* (Woburn Press, 1975)

——, *Oversubscribed: The Story of Highbury Grove* (Ward Lock Educational, 1974)

——, *Speaking My Mind: An Autobiography* (Peter Owen, 1995)

Brunner, Michael S., *Retarding America: The Imprisonment of Potential* (Halcyon House, Portland, Oregon, 1993)

Burchill, John, *Inspecting Schools: Breaking the Monopoly* (CPS, 1991)

Burn, John, and Colin Hart, *The Crisis in Religious Education* (Educational Research Trust, 1988)

Caldwell, Brian J., *The Promise of Self-Management for Schools: An International Perspective* (IEA Education Unit, 1987)

Chall, Jean S., *Learning to Read: The Great Debate* (McGraw-Hill, 1983)

Chew, Jennifer, *Literacy, Leeds, LINC and the Mixed Methods Myth* (CRE, 1992)

——, *Spelling Rules . . . OK* (CRE, 1992)

——, *Spelling Standards and Examination Results Among Sixth Formers, 1984–1990* (CRE, 1990)

Conference '90: Which History, Whose Values, What Culture, Illiteracy and Primary School Matters (CRE, 1990)

Cox, C., and R. Scruton, *Peace Studies: A Critical Survey* (IEDSS, 1984)

Cox, C., et. al., *Whose Schools? A Radical Manifesto* (The Hillgate Group, 1986)

Cox, Caroline, and John Marks, *The Insolence of Office* (The Claridge Press, 1988)

Cox, Caroline, Robert Balchin and John Marks, *Choosing a State School* (Century Hutchinson, 1989)

CRE, *Professional Expertise and Parental Experience in the Teaching of Reading or Mother Often Knows Best* (CRE, 1994)

124

Further Reading

Crowe, Gill, *Preparing Your Child for School* (from G. Crowe, 62 Kilsby Road, Barby, Rugby, Warwicks.)

Dennis, Norman, and George Erdos, *Families Without Fatherhood* (IEA, 1992)

Dennis, Norman, *Rising Crime and the Dismembered Family* (IEA, 1993)

Dennison, S. R., *Choice in Education* (IEA, 1986)

Deuchar, Stewart (ed.), *What Is Wrong With Our Schools?* (CRE, 1989)

——, *History on the Brink* (CRE, 1992)

——, *The New History: A Critique* (CRE, 1988)

Flew, Antony, *All the Right Places* (Adam Smith Institute, 1995)

——, *Power to the Parents: Reversing Educational Decline* (The Sherwood Press, 1987)

Hart, Colin E., *RE: Changing the Agenda* (The Christian Institute, Newcastle upon Tyne, 1994)

Hillgate Group, *The Reform of British Education – From Principles to Practice* (The Claridge Press, 1987)

Hiskett, Mervyn, *Choice in Rotten Apples: Bias in GCSE and Examining Groups* (CPS, 1988)

Hoskisson, John, *Positive Teaching: A Straightforward Guide to Success in the Classroom* (Danne Books, 1994)

Howson, Geoffrey, *Maths Problems: Can More Pupils Reach Higher Standards?* (CPC, 1989)

Ivens, Katie, and Nick Seaton, *Operation Whole Curriculum: A Tangled Web* (CRE, 1990)

Jager Adams, Marilyn, *Beginning to Read: Thinking and Learning About Print* (University of Illinois, 1990)

Lamb, Bernard C., *A National Survey of Communications Skills of Young Entrants to Industry and Commerce* (QES, 1993)

——, *A National Survey of Undergraduates' Standards of English* (QES, 1992)

Lawlor, Sheila, *Away with LEAs* (CPS, 1988)

——, *Correct Core: Simple Curricula for English, Maths and Science* (CPS, 1988)

——, *Opting Out: A Guide to Why and How* (CPS, 1988)

——, *Teachers Mistaught: Training in Theories or Education in Subjects* (CPS, 1990)

Lea, Ruth, and Desmond Boyle, *Education: IoD Business Option Survey* (Institute of Directors, London, 1996)

Letwin, Oliver, *Aims of Schooling: The Importance of Grounding* (CPS, 1988)

MacDonald, T. H., *First Aid in Reading, Writing and Spelling* (MacDonald, Hale and Iremonger, 1984 and 1988)

MacDonald, Theodore, *Much Ado About Reading (and How to Solve the Problem)* (CRE, 1992)

Maclure, Stuart, *Education Re-formed* (Hodder & Stoughton, 1988)

Marenbon, John, *English Our English – The New Orthodoxy Examined* (CPS, 1987)

Marks, John, *Standards in Schools: Assessment, Accountability and the Purposes of Education* (SMF, 1991)

——, *Value for Money in Education: Opportunity Costs and the Relationship Between Standards and Resources* (CRE, 1992)

Marsland, David, *Towards the Renewal of British Education* (CRE, 1992)

McNee, Mona, *Anybody Can Teach Reading If* (Mona McNee, 2 The Crescent, Toftwood, East Dereham, NR19 1NR, 1988)

——, *Anybody Can Teach Reading: Step by Step* (Mona McNee, as above)

——, *Learn Your Letter with Teddy* (Mona McNee, as above, 1988)

——, *You Can Write About Teddy* (Mona McNee, as above, 1988)

Morris, Joyce, *The Morris-Montessori Word List* (London Montessori Centre, 1990)

Naylor, Fred, *Technical Schools – A Tale of Four Countries* (CPS, 1985)

Norcross, Lawrence, and Peter Brown, *GCSE: The Egalitarian Fallacy and The Lost Battle* (IEA Education Unit, 1990)

North, Joanna (ed.), *The GCSE: An Examination* (The Claridge Press, 1987)

O'Hear, Anthony, *Education and Democracy: Against the Educational Establishment* (The Claridge Press, 1991)

——, *Father of Child-Centredness: John Dewey and the Ideology of Modern Education* (CPS, 1991)

——, *Who Teaches the Teachers?* (SAU, 1988)

O'Keeffe, Dennis, *The Wayward Curriculum* (SAU, 1986)

——, *The Wayward Elite* (Adam Smith Institute, 1990)

Riches, Valerie, *Sex and Social Engineering* (Family & Youth Concern, Wicken, Milton Keynes, MK19 6BU)

Scruton, R., A. Ellis-Jones and D. O'Keeffe, *Education and Indoctrination* (ERC, 1985)

Scruton, R., *World Studies: Education or Indoctrination?* (IEDDS, 1985)

Seaton, Nick (ed.), *Higher Standards and More Choice: A Manifesto for Our Schools* (CRE, 1992)

Further Reading

Seldon, Arthur, *The Riddle of the Voucher* (IEA, 1986)

Sexton, Stewart (ed.), *GCSE: A Critical Analysis* (IEA Education Unit, 1988)

Shaw, Beverley, *Comprehensive Schooling* (Basil Blackwell, 1983)

Stoll, Patricia, and Dennis O'Keeffe, *Officially Present* (IEA Education Unit, 1989)

The Teaching of Reading in 45 Inner London Primary Schools (Office for Standards in Education, London, 1996)

Tooley, James, *Education Without the State* (IEA, 1996)

Towards Employability: Addressing the Gap Between Young People's Qualities and Employers' Recruitment Needs (Industry in Education, 1996)

Turner, Martin, *Sponsored Reading Failure* (IPSET Education Unit, 1990)

White, Margaret (ed. J. Bogle), *Children and Contraception* (Order of Christian Unity, London, 1994)

Woodhead, Chris, *A Question of Standards: Finding the Balance* (Politeia, 1995)

Yeo, Ellen, *The Rise and Fall of Primary Education* (CRE, 1991)